LOSING BIG WINNING BIGGER

Learnings From Failure

SUJAY SANTRA

STARDOM BOOKS

www.StardomBooks.com

STARDOM BOOKS
A Division of Stardom Publishing
and infoYOGIS Technologies.
105-501 Silverside Road
Wilmington, DE 19809

Copyright © 2022 by Sujay Santra

This book is copyright under the Berne Convention.
No reproduction without permission.
All rights reserved.

The right of Sujay Santra to be identified as the author of this work has been asserted by him in accordance with sections 77 and 78 of the Copyright, Designs and Patents Act, 1988.

FIRST EDITION JULY 2022

STARDOM BOOKS

A Division of Stardom Alliance
105-501 Silverside Road Wilmington, DE 19809,
USA

www.stardombooks.com

Stardom Books, United States
Stardom Books, India

The author and publishers have made all reasonable efforts to contact copyright-holders for permission, and apologize for any omissions or errors in the form of credits given. Corrections may be made to future editions.

LOSING BIG WINNING BIGGER/
Learnings from failure

Sujay Santra

p. 186
cm. 13.5 X 21.5

Category:
BUS107000: Business & Economics : Personal Success
SEL027000: Self-Help : Personal Growth - Success

ISBN: 978-1-957456-11-9

DEDICATION

This book is dedicated to my late father, Shri Subhas Chandra Santra, who is still blessing me for all my endeavors. I hope this book guides a few souls the same way my father has been guiding me.

CONTENTS

ACKNOWLEDGMENTS   i

INTRODUCTION   1

PART A: A CURIOUS CASE CALLED LIFE   5

1. CHASED BY THE DOGS   7
2. PERSUASION IS THE ONLY IMPRESSION   25
3. PULL YOURSELF OUT OF THE DARK PIT   45
4. FINDING A BEST FRIEND IN A STRANGER   61
5. A SALARY OF IDLI VADA   79

PART B: A FAIL-PROOF PLAN TO SURVIVE   97

6. CATCHING THE BUS   99
7. AWAKEN THE DON WITHIN YOU   115
8. NOT ALL CLOUDS RAIN   131
9. STAYING CALM: A PRICELESS MANTRA   147
10. BAD PHASES: JUST A FEW PAUSES   159

CONCLUSION   171

ACKNOWLEDGMENTS

An entrepreneur's journey is challenging and lonely at the top. The road is bumpy, but you can never realize that in advance. While not all can share this ride with you, I was lucky to find support from some of the noble souls who embraced me by their virtue of grit and persistence. This book will be incomplete without a note of gratitude to them.

To begin with, I owe my mother for raising me for who I am today. Thank you, Maa, for trusting my instincts. I thank my daughter Ayushi and wife Sarah, who understood my true purpose in life and supported my big mission. Their unwavering support always makes me stronger.

A special note for Pritha Chatterjee and Shirsha Bhattacharjee, who remained a sounding board while I crafted my narrative for the younger breeds. Their enthusiasm was electrifying as they were always eager to chip in beyond their working hours. I thank Debaleena Ganguly for her lively creative illustrations. It was fascinating to witness her creative skills come alive to the world. I also thank Dr. Tirumala for being by my side whenever I needed her. My Stardom partners were like my anchors. I thank Ranjitha and Atrayee, who believed in my story and pushed me to wear the author's hat.

It is hard to find selfless people in today's busy world. But I was fortunate to find support from the very learned and respectable people who were always there for me. I want to thank Jayesh Bhai, Sunder, Nandan, BS Rao, Dr. Judy and Dr. Debashis for their unconditional support. Entrepreneurs thrive due to who they know but not what they know. I have been part of the global networking forum which includes Ashoka Changemakers, MIT Cambridge, Miller Center, & Rotarians, where I could learn the brass tacks of handling challenges, the power of resilience in the face of disruption and could discover the power of purpose.

A special mention to Swadeep, Somatish, Bishweshwar, and Pritha Chakraborty, who inspired me to attain challenging goals. Friends and well-wishers are the lifelines of entrepreneurs. Those who build start-ups face the rigors alone, but creating a support system balances work and stress. I thank my 3 AM childhood buddies Nayan, Avik and Shraboni, for supporting my endeavors. I also thank my well-wishers, Nishi Ji, Himabindu, Todd and Mikunj, because of whom I found stability and connections.

The critical ingredients to building a well-functioning team include acquiring, building and nurturing. My team complements my ability to drive motivation, purpose and mission. I thank members who stood as solid pillars, Biltu, Uddip, Sandip, Ria and Avipsa, for creating a solid foundation for the new members to learn and follow. I also thank Sanoop for driving the tech team, championing optimism against adversity, and the ground team members, including Tapan, Mintu and Annada, for their steadfast commitment during uncertain times.

This book will help the rockstar youth and the lost souls to navigate through the rocky road and will make them understand that losing big is as crucial as winning bigger.

Happy Reading!

INTRODUCTION

In current times, life is moving at a different pace, dancing to a different rhythm. Everything is about the millennials; a generation which is unique in its perception, attitude and the very way they face life and its unpredictable challenges. The millennials are unlike any other generation. Flourishing amidst the power of digitization, they are spoilt for choice as there exists a plethora of options for them to succeed in life. But more choices bring many more challenges. With so many options to grow and succeed in hand, millennials are somehow obsessed with boasting about their success stories. The power of internet and social network has made them global citizens. They are so infatuated with the virtual world that they are gradually losing touch with the real world. They often forget that life is uncertain and thrives on the premise of unpredictability. A dawn that shines with the glory of success may end in a gloomy dusk of failures. Today's boastful success story may die an untimely death.

No matter how powerful or successful we are, we can never have a complete control over life. Every dawn will knock at our door with challenges and we have to chalk out a plan to deal with them, overcome them and move ahead towards our goal. The real picture of life is at total variance with the virtual world that rules the internet. The scholars call life competitive; the doers find life exciting due to its challenges.

But then there is a whole clan which is falling prey to the constant oscillation between success and failure. We often measure success and celebrate it because history honors only the victors. However, does that mean that there is an escape route to avoid failures? No. Failures make some interesting chapters in our success story. Failures open a new door towards learning something new, something never thought of.

In our pursuit of success, we often forget that unless we fall flat, we can never learn to get up. There will be days when we will be chased out by the brutality of life and then there will be a new beginning with immense courage to face every challenge. And that is what life is all about. Some days we will take refuge inside a depressed mind not knowing that a stranger might help us in coming out of that unfathomable pit of depression. Failed interviews, unthought of setbacks in academics, broken relationships, bullying at workplaces, unwarranted embarrassment and the list goes on and on. Challenges come in a new avatar every single day and there is no other way but to face them strategizing our moves to overcome them.

When life is competitive and making money becomes the ultimate objective, young minds are allured to entrepreneurship. Consumed by the idea of becoming their own boss, the younger generation fails to see the real struggle behind building a business. The repeated grinds, sleepless nights, compromised meals, regular emotional harassment – they all are a part and parcel of a successful life. As millennials indulge in admiring the glamorous lives of entrepreneurs, they blissfully forget to see the reality of life. The real world is brutal, erratic and always ready to pounce upon us.

However, in the midst of this pandemonium of success and failure, growth happens. Mind matures with challenges and when we learn to celebrate failures, we learn the untaught lessons of life. Life is a motley of good and bad phases where none gets a permanent residence. It is a loop and we all swing between joy and grief while embracing the only constant factor of life i.e., change.

Life is about transition and in every step, we make new arrangements to carve a niche for ourselves. We are not bestowed with the power to choose between success and failure but we are indeed given the ability to learn, unlearn and relearn and win big. So, are you afraid of failures? Are you cocooned inside the deepest den of depression? Are you mesmerized by the façade of the virtual world?

Fear Not! It is absolutely okay to fail or get trapped inside an illusion of success. The real essence of success does not rest at the pinnacle but lies in the process of reaching the goal. Before you think of giving up, let me take you on an honest journey of life where failures indeed make the stepping stones to success.

PART A

A CURIOUS CASE CALLED LIFE

1

CHASED BY THE DOGS

IT WAS 3 AM!

Tucked in the sweet embrace of a fading night, I was walking back home. Dark, bereft of any life around, and still, the cold had a kind of warmth around it. I looked at the sky – a delicate crescent of moon peeped at me from that lacy grey-edged cloud, and those stars shone as if grains of sugar were spilt on a black marble. Roads were windswept, so much so that I could hear a mild breeze lugging on to me. Delhi still seemed to be lounging in the world of dreams. And here I was, at the brink of dawn, walking back from my office, from Qutab Enclave to Jiya Sarai.

The whole ambience seemed animated as my footsteps knocked at my ears. I could hear my breathing and could feel the blood rushing through my veins too. It wasn't anything new. There have been countless nights when I had to jump over the boundary wall of IIT Delhi to take a shortcut to my house. Everything was as if encoded in my mind. I had nothing to worry. My feet would automatically turn towards the wall, and I would climb and jump on the other side. That's it. It was as simple as it sounded.

I wondered about one programming task that I had been working during the day and climbed on the wall. However, before I could jump to the other side, I was startled by a pack of dogs. Their ears pinned back, baring teeth and growling; those sharp canines glistened amidst the darkness. Standing on the ledge of the wall, I could feel fear stabbing at my spine. What should I do? Should I rush back to my office? No! I took out my belt and jumped in front of those dogs. And before they could pounce on me, I began to swing the belt in every direction. The dogs kept barking and chased me as far as they could but I didn't stop or let my fear take over me. I kept my belt business on until I reached home.

Does it sound foolish? Could I not escape this episode of being chased by the dogs? Obviously, I could. It would have been far easier and safer for me to take a walk back to my office and relax in my cozy, dog-free cabin. However, life wouldn't have been so memorable without the surge of courage that night. Hounded by those barking canines, the night made me realize one crucial aspect of life – The only thing certain in life is its uncertainty! The most atrocious and yet precious gift of life is its uncertainty.

Though it comes with the façade of fear, uncertainty in life does sow the seeds of hope. I could have never imagined getting ringed by a pack of drooling dogs, that too in the middle of the night in a windswept street. I never knew that I had the guts to face that sudden and unexpected event in life. However, as days passed by, I fathomed the very significance of life's uncertainty. Only because it is uncertain, anything, absolutely anything is possible. Life has its own quirky ways to introduce us to our inherent potential.

Life is bound to give you unexpected results as it clings on to a designer garb of uncertainty. Future runs on the treadmill of ambiguity, and no matter how many astrologers proclaim to have a control over it, future prediction is never possible. If future would have been predictable, all those astrologers would have minted money in the stock market. We all want a perfect ending. However, life is busy messing it up.

We are bound to get poems that don't rhyme, stories that never make a good ending and we would never know when the script is introducing a dramatic change. But does that mean, life is meaningless? No. Ambiguity is delicious, for it brews hope in the cauldron of uncertainties. Instead of pursuing a perfect life, we can actually unleash our inner strength amidst this chaos of uncertainty.

As Albert Einstein once quoted, "*As far as the laws of mathematics refer to reality, they are not certain; and as far as they are certain, they do not refer to reality.*" Uncertainty is the very essence of all life and that is the only reality. We obviously long for clarity of goals and try to make immaculate plans. Nevertheless, we do harbor a fascination towards the unpredictable future. We are overjoyed when a chance occurrence bestows us with something unexpectedly flattering. However, as soon as life dismisses our plans, our confidence shatters, wisdom wanes and pragmatism fails. Why? Because our plan was unidirectional. We were neither prepared for the worst nor had we conceived a Plan B. Failure doesn't hurt as much as the unpredictability of success does. We often fall prey to our one-dimensional approach towards life. Either we tend to over-nourish our confidence or we just fail to be flexible in our goals.

Let's take the example of an IIT aspirant. Rohit was a young boy, extremely good in Mathematics and Physics. He had always aspired to be an IIT graduate and his preparation was ceaseless for the same. He was confident of his abilities and was determined to crack the entrance at one go.

However, on the day of the entrance exam, he faced a terrible accident on his way to the examination center. He couldn't appear for the exam. Heartbroken by this unfortunate incident, he lost confidence over a period of time. The next year, though he could appear for the entrance exam, his performance was not up to the mark and he failed to clear. Joining IIT soon became a love's labor's lost as he failed in his next attempt too. All this while, the young lad, though extremely good at mathematics, didn't realize that instead of focusing only on IIT, he could have easily secured a place in other prestigious institutions.

After 3 failed attempts, when he finally decided to abandon his IIT dream and join a regular graduation course, he was 3 years senior to the present lot of applicants. The system didn't see his trials and tribulations with IIT dream. All it did was to consider him a student who had taken a long break. He was categorized under college dropouts.

What do you think of Rohit? I would call him a warrior without a plan. He was good at his game; he knew the tactics but he hadn't planned well enough to move ahead. We are humans, God's greatest creation. We chase our dreams and work to fulfill our aspirations to make our life better and more fulfilling. However, most of the times we are not prepared for the untimely adversities of life. Consider life as a very strict teacher who is famous for taking surprise tests. As soon as we program our brain for such surprise tests, we win half the battle. Fear of uncertainty adds to stress on our brain and nothing else. Believe me, nobody knows how to live. There is no secret mantra to live a perfect life as perfection remains the biggest illusion around us. Life is simply lived in the shadow of uncertainty while we keep collecting myriad of experiences. Some of these experiences are brightly hued, painted with joy and success, while others loom over our head as 'lessons learnt'.

Honestly, human beings crave for information about the future in the same way they desire food, sex, and other primary rewards. Our brains perceive ambiguity as a threat, and they try to protect us by diminishing our ability to focus on anything other than certainty. Can you believe that job uncertainty poses a bigger threat to our health that the actual loss of job? The worst situation poses less threat to our mind than the fear of the situation turning worse. In one of the psychological experiments, it was found that the people who were told that they had a 50% chance of receiving a painful electric shock felt far more anxious and agitated than the people who were certain about receiving the shocks. I often wonder at those gigantic industries that devote their time and energy to filling in the blanks of our futures. Do we not see huge hoardings of astrologers or future shapers looming large in the crowded spaces of our cities?

In fact, there are many popular astrology apps that claim to change your future with a click. We are thrown a pandemonium of strategies to combat uncertainty. No? On one hand, fundamentalist religions provide unambiguous rules and absolute truths to combat fear of uncertainty, while conspiracy theories take a U-turn over simple explanations for various phenomena.

In all probability, *"Uncertainty is the only certainty there is,"* as proclaimed by John Allen Paulos. In our efforts towards evolving as the best creation of God, our brains were rigged to resist uncertainty. No matter how many astrologers shriek about their planetary acumen, no one can ever predict the future. Let me ask you this - Before the Covid pandemic massively disrupted our routines and utterly destroyed our best-laid plans, could anyone predict it? No! Global shutdown, businesses hitting the skids, millions losing their jobs and lives, all was beyond anyone's wildest dreams. Since the outbreak, all we could do was to take precautions. While the news channels kept yelping at the rising death rate, we could chalk out an alternative plan to fit inside the new normal. When the offices didn't open and the businesses had to run, Zoom came in as an escape route. When school doors were shut for the children, classrooms assumed the shape and size of mobile screens. When wearing a mask became the new dress code, designer houses started offering matching masks with the apparel.

We can never determine or control the uncertainty of life. Knowing how to live with insecurity is the only security we have as humans and we have to script our own dictionary to find meaning in chaos.

Cut A Deal With Uncertainty

Life is throwing challenges at every nook and corner. My entrepreneurial endeavor has been recognized by someone like Shri. Ratan Tata. My company has come under an esteemed umbrella of a person who is God to every young Indian dreaming of a glorious business. I am indebted, overjoyed and of course grateful. But does that mean that I have become immune to challenges? Never. As I went through my highs and lows, I learned one essential element of living life peacefully. I can never control life and its idiosyncrasies. However, can I not control my responses? I have had my share of terrible failures and I too had episodes where I was left with nothing but hopelessness.

However, as I learned to hold the reins of my emotions, I could sail through the tide. The more we bog down, the more overpowering will the extraneous factors be. There is no point in resisting uncertainty as resistance can never help us recover, learn, grow, or feel better. The irony is, resistance prolongs our pain and difficulty by amplifying the challenging emotions we are feeling. There is a brutal truth to Jung's observation that whatever you resist persists.

So, what should we do when life seems unfair to us? Instead of resisting, we can practice acceptance. You won't believe that the secret to my happiness is nothing but acceptance. Acceptance is about meeting life where it is and moving forward from there. As we accept the situation around, we get to see a prismatic effect on the reality. Every ingredient of the present situation looks crystal clear. And soon, we get out of our paralyzed fearful mindset and move forward in life. So how could I practice acceptance? I surrendered my power to resist a problematic situation and stopped feeding my emotion of fear.

Let me take you back to Rohit. With every failed attempt, Rohit tried hard on physical level. However, his emotions were unrestrained. They were still chained with the fear of failure. I am sure, all of you have watched the movie called '3 Idiots'. Sometimes, we just have to move with the flow without thrusting unnecessary pressure on us. Nobody is immune to failure, but how we deal with failure is what makes us stand apart. Nobody can resist a bad situation from happening. All we can do is to channelize our thoughts towards the solution instead of harping on the problem.

Let's say, you are a young couple and your marriage is gradually falling apart. Both of you are unable to give time to each other in your race to achieve career goals. Times turn challenging and you end up criticizing and blaming each other. However, as days pass by, you realize that instead of finding faults in each other, it is better to keep calm and give some time to the relationship. In short, you accept that something is wrong and instead of letting the world know about it, you decide to take each day at a time.

Will it resolve your marital dispute? No. Will you start feeling less frustrated or disappointed? Yes. Because you are no longer striving to make everything alright at one go. You acknowledge the existence of the problem and slowly start moving on with the problem to find a solution. We have to understand that acceptance is not equal to resignation. Accepting a situation doesn't mean that you need not work towards something that can improve the present scenario. Do you know what the real problem with our mind and emotions is?

As soon as we encounter a defect or problem, we jump the gun that hell has broken lose on us and nothing good can ever happen henceforth. We fail to realize that the only thing that remains constant is change. If good days are bound to fade away, bad days are going to follow the same route. This power of accepting the situation cannot be injected inside you. It MUST brew within. You shall script stories of success and also the fables of failures. It is inevitable. Most of the people around you shall take refuge to pitying you on your failures. Sit and ponder for once, do those pitying eyes ever help you to come out of your defeat? No. Never.

Fix this in your mind - you are the best resource to unleash your potential. If you can get a proper grip over your waning emotions, you can brace yourself against uncertainty. You are your resource to craft your success story. There will be times when life will grind you with unfortunate moments. However, never let your resources deplete and fall prey to the hurdles. Never underinvest in your body, mind and soul. It is indeed okay to fail. Nobody is immune to failure and failure is not fatal. Nevertheless, if you are capable of channeling your emotions in a positive way, you can become unstoppable. It's you who has to churn out the power and courage to take life head on.

This century has witnessed geniuses like Bill Gates, Jeff Bezos and likes, who could really bring any kind of ball in their court. Was it sheer luck that they could excel in life? No success ever comes with just the luck in your favor. You could have been born with a silver spoon and yet fall hard on the ground. None of us can escape the unfavorable turn of events.

In the current times, when India is baking entrepreneurs from every stratum of life, Elon Musk remains an absolute inspiration to every young dreamer. It is like whatever ideas crop up in Musk's mind are nothing less than revolutionary. He had once stated that he often had so many ideas that he struggled to focus on one project. He is a successful entrepreneur, innovator, and one of the richest people in the world with a net worth crossing multibillion dollar. In fact, he is among the top 10 of the world's wealthiest people as one of his companies, Tesla boomed during the COVID-19 pandemic. It is important to highlight that Musk too had faced failure on multiple occasions under controversial circumstances. He, however, emerged from dark and miserable times in flying colors.

When Elon first started out, he had applied to a number of emerging tech companies including Netscape. He was rejected, and in view of these rejections, he founded a searchable business directory called Zip2, which was essentially an online version of a telephone book. It wasn't a simple idea back then when the use of computers was still very low. Unfortunately, Zip2 struggled in the early years and Elon couldn't find investors to fund his way out. Later, Musk wrote the code for a mapping project which enabled him to combine the two ideas. It is noteworthy that the company staff lived on office premises to cut down on costs.

It was 1996 when Zip2 received the much-needed investment, but Musk was ousted as the CEO of the company and given a much smaller role. It didn't take him long to remove the later CEO, Richard Sorkin, when the latter projected a different vision for the company. Zip2 garnered considerable success and Musk decided to move on and work on a brand-new concept that was the beginning of what we now know as PayPal. Even PayPal was considered a disastrous business proposal when the idea was conceived. It nevertheless became a success. How? It turns out that Elon Musk has this incredible ability to adjust when necessary and he seeks to create a product that provides a clear solution to the end-user. Similarly, the naysayers threw mud over Tesla but it is now one of the most successful producers of electric cars.

Why am I sharing these stories with you? It is because none of this would have been possible had Musk not persevered. It was Elon Musk's firm belief in his ideas that converted them into such gigantic success stories. Today Elon Musk is a living example of the fact that working on a personal passion is arguably the most powerful driving force that anyone can have. Life will never lay blossoms on your path. It is not going to cajole you when you stumble and fall apart. Life is going to push you farther towards the dark mines and it is entirely your decision if you wish to weep over the dark coal or choose to dig the diamond out of it.

Keep Your Plan B Ready

Have you ever baked a cake? Let's say you have recently undergone some baking classes and to celebrate the completion of your course, you decide to throw a tea party to your friends. You plan to treat your guests with a handmade cake. You handpick all the ingredients carefully from the supermarket and voila! You are all set to surprise everyone with a delicious cranberry cake. Oven set, ingredients measured and mixed, and the power goes off as soon as you start the hand-blender.

Oh! Never mind. You can always mix and whip everything in the old school style. It is going to be a little tiring, still, worth the effort. Hours pass by and there is no sign of power supply. You look at the clock and the minute hand seem to move faster than usual. What should you do now? Mio Amore is on the next street. You could always get a cake from there or you could order something from Zomato and put the baking project at the backburner. Instead of changing the core plan of surprising your friends with your newly gained skill, you opt for a Plan B. You follow your grandma's style of baking a cake in the pressure cooker. No power, no worries!

There is always a Plan B. You must ensure a Plan B in place before you plunge into anything in life. What if you fail to clear an entrance exam? Does it mean you don't have any future in life?

Whenever you feel stuck in life and see everything going upside down, google about the successful entrepreneurs of the world. A failure didn't stop them, they rather got hold of the failure to dissect out the flaws. If you complain of the uncertainties of life, realize that there lies an opportunity in every uncertainty. If you falter and fail to find the ray of light at the end of the tunnel, you just have to move on and on further into the tunnel till you finally reach the end.

Now, if the 'cake baking - power cut' scenario looks too commonplace to highlight the pain of uncertainty, let me build another scene to prove my point. What if you have everything ready, but the dried cranberry curdles the cream? All efforts gone waste. Whether you bake such a cake in your newly bought OTG or in the pressure cooker, it is going to have a bad taste. Now what? You are in tears, not knowing what to do. The option of Mio Amore is still open. But then, you open your fridge and find a big box of cream cheese, all intact and inviting. What do you do? You grind some crackers, blend the cream cheese, add the cranberries and there you serve an awesome, lip-smacking cheesecake to your guests. The point is, somewhere, at some nook or corner, the same uncertain life is peeking out with a Plan B. It's we who have to be watchful and flexible enough to change.

I have seen the problems that can crop up in the absence of a Plan B. A few years ago, a friend of mine took a plunge into entrepreneurship after serving a decade in the corporate world. He had a great idea for his startup and could secure funding quite easily. He was so overjoyed with the smooth processing that he went to the next step of hiring a team, marketing the business in Brazil and blah blah. However, things didn't move the way he had expected them to. Though everything was sanctioned on paper, funding didn't reach his pocket. My friend went through a terrible time with creditors stalking him every now and then. The recruits too shared the bad blood; friends and peers looked at him as if he had stolen their wallets. One could see the stress in his eyes as he struggled with the untoward situation. Within a few months' time, I could see my friend losing out on his confidence terribly. Why?

Because more than the unexpected situation, he was haunted by the absence of Plan B. He had never expected his plans to fail so miserably in the market. He was so certain about the success of his venture, that he completely overlooked the need for an alternative.

Never lose sight of the necessity and benefits of a Plan B. Investing your ideas into an alternative solution is more like self-care. It is like erecting a barrier to an emotional breakdown. Sticking to only one course of action not only makes you inflexible, but also self-centered. Just like myopia is not good for our eyes, a myopic vision towards your goal actually hinders your progress. It's 21st century and life is moving at a supersonic speed. If one movie clicks and makes you the next Shah Rukh Khan, that doesn't mean you can keep on doing the same kind of movie again and again. We all thrive with the sole purpose to succeed in life. Keeping that goal in mind, we must chalk out our plans. On the same note, none of your plans can be failure-proof. Every plan, whether A or Z, has its own set of flaws, but does that mean we should stop trying? If you remain pigheaded towards your approach, then nothing can protect you from this uncertain life. You have to understand that uncertainty is the inherent nature of life and we have to embrace life with all its blind alleys and surprise turns.

Chaos Is Not Meaningless

Uncertainty disturbs our mental state. It leaves us with nothing but undue stress and anxiousness. To combat these issues, flexibility is the key. If we are to stay flexible, we need to feel safe and secure. When we feel uncertain or insecure, our brain tries to rescue us by activating our dopamine system. This dopamine rush encourages us to seek rewards, making temptations more tempting. Think of this as your brain pushing you toward a comfort item, may be like a piece of dark chocolate or a cup of hot coffee.

I am sure, many of you would end up binging on pizzas whenever you have a bad day at the office. In fact, shopping helps. But does it make the uncertain situation vanish?

No. They all serve as a distraction, that is, it's your brain's way to let you know that life is not over with one unexpected turn of events. Similarly, a lot of things happen around every day. Your neighbor may die all of a sudden at the age of 40 or your brother may lose to his colleague over a promotion. These sudden changes do affect our inner well-being, although we are not directly involved in the process. Instead of going into the nutshell of probabilities, we have to learn to distance ourselves from the negative thoughts. Just as death is normal, losing a chance of promotion is normal too. Simply because people close to you have fallen prey to such uncertainty, it doesn't mean that the same is going to happen with you.

Whenever, you witness a change from the normalcy, it is better to prepare your mind to accept that change as normal. Learn from the experiences and design a better way to deal with it. It can be helpful for us to consider worst-case scenarios to weigh risks and actively prevent disaster. In case we start believing that the same thing will happen to us, we tend to react emotionally as though the worst thing is already happening to us in real life. What can be a better example than the Covid pandemic hoarding scenario?

Many across the world hoarded food, toiletries, sanitizers and even oxygen cylinders. Everything happened due to a false presumption of what if there is no sanitizer tomorrow; what if I don't get an oxygen cylinder when I get infected. Quite often we grieve for things that we haven't actually lost, and react to events that are not actually happening in our life. The more we let our thoughts rule our mind, the more vulnerable we become. Unexpected incidents do make us feel threatened, afraid, and unsafe.

However, as soon as we alter our emotions to achieve our bigger goal, we are braced to face the uncertain life. Think but Do Not Ruminate! Our bias towards negativity often sets us up for failure. Our expectations are self-fulfilling prophecy.

When we expect the worst, we feel too afraid or close-minded to seize opportunities or respond to challenges with creativity and grit. Instead of buying into every stressful thought, can we not actively imagine the best possible scenario?

There remains a silver lining hidden somewhere, and as we take a cleaner lens to look at the situation, we overcome our natural tendency to overestimate risks and negative consequences. Instead of imagining a scary and unknown future, we can bring our attention to our breath and establish a connect with our inner self.

The fear of failure debilitates us and everything that is out of our control scares the hell out of us. Do you know that Steven Spielberg was thrown out of film school thrice? Albert Einstein was called 'mentally slow' by his teachers. Why to go far? Sourav Ganguly, one of the finest captains of Indian Cricket Team, was removed from captaincy. In the year 2005, Ganguly was dropped from the ODI team and by January 2006, he was removed from the test squad as well. Today however, Sourav Ganguly is the President of BCCI. So, is it like all these celebrities never felt bogged down? Huh! Ganguly would have spent hundreds of sleepless nights wondering what he had not done right. A renowned newspaper had the audacity to publish a photo showing him concentrating on his bat's sticker. Do you think Ganguly could ignore it? No.

There is nothing called ignorance when you are criticized on a public forum. I am sure he had never expected to have been treated like that. But things happened and he could have no control over them. The only thing he could control was his response to adversity. If you attend to what is happening within you at any given moment, it will keep a check on the external reality affecting your inner truth. It will allow you to cultivate calm, open-mindedness, and non-reactivity.

We all are preyed upon by situations which make us feel powerless. We get trapped in narratives that leave us feeling angry, helpless, and confused. Instead of rekindling the power within us, we often seek refuge in others. It certainly feels good when someone cares for us and sympathizes with our misery. But believe me, this dependence on others is as hollow as a bird's bone because the very people you depend on to help you out will take charge of your life. No one can enter your shoes.

If you wish to brace yourself against uncertainty, surround yourself with people who can support your emotions and unveil your true potential. When we take responsibility for our lives, we trade the false power of victimhood for the real power that comes from creating the life we want.

I could unleash the true meaning of chaos in life when I went to deliver a lecture at MIT, Boston. Guided by the weather forecast, I had carried just a thermal wear with me. Just before the landing of the flight, a snowstorm struck and the temperature slipped down to (−)6 degrees. I didn't know what to do. Shivering due to the sudden drop in temperature, I checked my watch. My talk was in another 2 hours and no shop was open for me to buy another set of warm jackets. I had never faced such a biting winter in my life before. Also, I could not afford to miss the chance of delivering a lecture on such a prestigious podium. I could have left everything behind to take shelter inside the warmth of airport, but then, I would have lost the golden opportunity to speak before the MIT students. Believe me when I say this, I still don't know from where I got the spirit to reach the MIT campus in that single thermal coat.

Nobody had injected any special serum into me to combat the cold. There were hundreds of passengers who preferred to wait until the snowstorm stopped. But, I didn't. For me, giving a speech at MIT was far more precious than protecting myself from the cold. I still remember a student named Catherine. She saw me penning down my notes wearing that flimsy jacket and got her husband's coat for me. The coat was certainly for a bigger man but I wore the given jacket and confidently claimed the dais.

Here, I am not trying to portray the I-Me-Myself scenario. My focus is on making you see that Life is going to throw you umpteen number of challenges but the power to make decisions still lies with you. Whether you bog down or fight back is entirely your choice. I lost my father on the 2nd of August, 2020. No matter how sick your loved one has been, you are never able to accept their death. I was terribly shaken by the tragedy. I had lost my father but had received the invitation for the lecture at CII at the same time.

I was torn between my grief at the loss of my father and the anxiety over jeopardizing the flow of events due to sudden cancellation of my lecture at MIT. My father had always taught me to put professionalism before everything else. Now that he wasn't with me anymore, I had to respect his teachings. I could never get my father back but could always be guided by his wisdom.

Everything in life may not happen for good – after all, seeing your father dying in front of your eyes can never be a good thing. However, there is always a hidden meaning in every chapter of life. Every word scripted in your life carries a hint of something better. Today, people cite that fateful incident to acknowledge my zest for professionalism even when faced with personal tragedy.

Tell me honestly, had you ever thought that MBA classes would happen over a zoom call? Could you ever guess that weekends would keep you locked up inside your houses? Never. In the last two years of the Covid pandemic, thousands of healthy people died while many octogenarians continued to live uninfected. The point is, life is fickle, moody, disruptive and challenging. It totally depends upon us how we choose to tackle it. Meaning and purpose are wellsprings of hope. When the world feels scary or uncertain, feeling a sense of purpose can ground us better than anything else. To best cope with uncertainty, we need to stop complaining. When we drop our fixation on the problem, we can focus on the outcomes we desire. We cannot simply wait for the ordeal to be over. Instead of anticipating for good times to come to us, we should accept, adapt and accommodate the changes happening around us.

Don't Let The Cat Out (Too Soon)

While flourishing in the era of insta-influencers, accept it or not, we have become obsessed with showing off.

You buy a new lipstick and your Display Picture ends up with a pout. You get a new job and there you paint your LinkedIn profile with company logo, welcome pack and what not. So, is there any harm in letting the world know about your success? Absolutely not.

Sharing always amplifies the essence of joy. The hitch however, lies in letting the cat out too soon. The real life is not about flaunting your new lipstick. When you are tangled in that inescapable web of social networking, you are pried by hundreds of people. Once you announce your little success, the whole virtual world looks up to you to continue with the flow of success. Now, is that possible? You are going to fail at some point or the other, and if that failure is disclosed in public, are you prepared to handle the criticism or unwarranted sympathy?

You may label my thoughts as old-fashioned that I don't prefer to disclose anything on social media or amongst the peers until everything is finalized. But, this one strategy has helped me to brace myself against the uncertainty of life. How? Am I superstitious that someone will put an evil eye on my success? No. It is a preventive measure to ensure that people around get to know more about me once I am assured of the happenings in my life.

Even today, I take pride in getting acknowledged by none other than Ratan Tata. However, I never disclosed the fact to anyone immediately. I took my own time to absorb the joy of my achievement, to bask in the glory in private before letting the world learn about it. So, before you share that big dream of yours with the world, let's understand the science-backed reasons why you may want to keep it to yourself if you want to reach that goal. In 2009, Peter Gollwitzer and his colleagues published a research paper suggesting that the simple act of sharing your goal publicly can make you less likely to do the work to achieve it. Researchers concluded that when someone acknowledges the value of your goal, that social recognition is a reward that may cause you to reduce your efforts.

A goal is often tied to your identity. A premature appreciation often makes your brain think that the job is half done, which is nothing but a glittering façade. You put an intriguing post about a burning situation on Facebook and garner a couple of likes. You go a step ahead and post a beautifully captured selfie, and you are flooded with likes, loves and hundreds of comments. Then onwards, you understand the trick of the game and start posting photos instead of concentrating on the basic premise of social networking. Your actual reason for being a part of a social network is lost in maintaining the façade and in a couple of months, you are tagged as an attention seeker with nothing good to offer to the world around.

Moreover, disclosing your idea to others is one way of attracting negative feedback. Are you prepared for that? What if you are an electrical engineer, but have got placed in a software company? You share the joy of getting the job while most receive the news with a raised brow – what will you do with computers? You share the joy of submitting your PhD dissertation thesis and everyone keeps coming to you asking to show your degree. What if the presentation gets delayed? What if your supervisor ends up asking for some major changes? It is not only about keeping a backup plan ready; it is also about revealing your plan only after analyzing the volatile feature of life.

"Uncertainty of the future gives us hope and keeps us humble. Since no one can be sure of what tomorrow brings, we can be hopeful without being boastful."
– Paul TP Wong

Although we are all travelling in the same train of life, we are destined for different stations. We all are given our own set of paints, canvas and spot to draw our success. Just as I was chased by those dogs, each one of you is going to face your nightmare at some point in time. Worry Not! Trust the process. Your mind shall walk you through your truest potential. While complaining about the uncertainty of life, we all get two choices. We can either feel depressed by the unexpected events in life or can wait for the WOW moments once the hurdles are overcome.

Our maturity lies in our ability to endure uncertainty, live in the moment and learn to accept change as a normal phenomenon. Uncertainty is indeed uncomfortable, but believe me certainty in life would bring more absurdity to it.

2

PERSUASION IS THE ONLY IMPRESSION

"Not brute force but only persuasion and faith are the kings of this world."
– Thomas Carlyle

What is the first thing that pops up in your head when I utter *persuasion*? It is a little difficult to decipher the true meaning of persuasion as we all invariably associate it with a negative behavior. It is more like an impish tactic to get your things done. As a child, you would have persuaded your parents to get you a brand-new cricket kit only because your best friend has got one. No? You would have nagged them every now and then to get you a bike on your birthday because it was more of a swag you wanted to flaunt within your friend circle. Persuasion is an art which we often synonymize with manipulation and tag the art of persuasion as another weapon of Loki. However, persuasion is a basic human skill to reach your goal. Your power of persuasion can build or wreck the premise of your student and professional life. If you wish to influence people with your ideology, you have to realize that your idea is a mere compass while your persuasion skill is the map to follow.

We all are inherently persuasive. It is a skill that humanity has nurtured to reach its goal. Let's have a peek into human persuasive nature through this slice of fiction.

Dhriti is a student of class 6, always distracted from her curriculum and an average performer in academics. Her school plans for a summer camp and she wishes to participate in the program. Her parents are dead against it because they think she will be all the more distracted from her studies. She argues, she cries, but none of her parents bend the rule. And then, one fine day, she chalks out a plan of negotiation. She has not been very good at Mathematics and has never scored enough to be in the gang of top-rankers.

She makes a proposition to her parents that if she scores more than 80% in Mathematics, they would allow her to go to the summer camp. After much deliberation, her parents agree because they are sure that scoring 80% in the said subject is not possible for Dhriti. However, Dhriti is so determined to join the camp that she puts her shoulder to the wheel and makes it happen. She scores 90/100 in her final examination and leaves everyone flabbergasted. Her parents are happy and can no longer stop her from taking what she wants.

So, is this a story of sheer determination? Partly yes and partly no. Her parents did not agree to her demands as they couldn't find her credible enough. Dhriti failed to convince her parents at first because she couldn't justify her demand. She rose to the occasion and brought a change in herself as she had promised. This fictional story proves that you cannot persuade people with hollow words; you must brace your verbal utterings with solid demonstrable actions.

Whether you are an engineering student trying to get your internship done in a famous company, or you are a new recruit in a big MNC, your persuasion skill will impact several aspects of job performance. Whether you are working with your friends on a school project, or you are running a startup, your ability to work in a team or lead a team heavily relies on the power of persuasion and the ability to influence others.

As I spent years building my business and network, my persuasion skill proved to be one of the most powerful tools in my toolshed. If my team is committed to or sold on the importance of my vision and long-term mission, it is because of my ability to persuade them to align their personal goals with the organizational goals.

It was one of those struggling days of my career. I was still fencing my entrepreneurial life and had been called by a leading surgeon from Durgapur. Excited and determined to grow my business, I decided to meet him in his hospital itself. Those days, there was no direct mode of transport from Kharagpur to Durgapur and I had to bargain over the fastest mode possible. The next day, I woke up at 4 AM and caught the first train to Bankura. From there, I reached Durgapur via bus. My meeting was scheduled for 8 AM in and it was 7:15 AM when I had reached the reception of that leading hospital. Thrilled and nervous in turns, I patiently waited for the surgeon to let me roll out my business proposal. Hours passed by and I still remained sitting, waiting for someone to give me a chance to explain the reason for my presence there. It was around 10 o'clock when one of the hospital staff informed me that the doctor was busy with a serious surgery and won't be available anytime soon. A little worried, I wondered what to do next. I considered going back without meeting the surgeon.

I was damn tired. Awake since 4 AM and travelling in local train and buses in those odd hours of the day wasn't an easy thing to do. A thought flashed through my mind - What would I do by going back to Kharagpur now? The hospital ambience was good, quite luxurious I would say, I could wait there without anyone bothering me. So, instead of troubling my legs again in the cramped bus or train, I decided to wait on in the hospital hall. The whole day passed by and around 6 in the evening, the doctor got free of his medical duties. When he looked at me, he was taken aback. He glanced at his watch and I couldn't understand if he was astonished at my patience or dismayed by my stubbornness. He invited me into his cabin to discuss my business proposal.

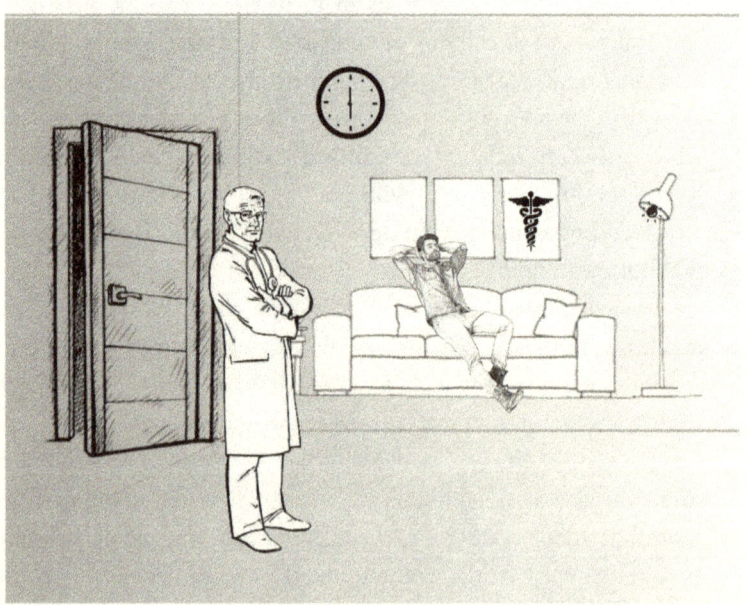

I had spoken for about half an hour when that esteemed surgeon invited me to have dinner with him at his house. I laid out my business proposal in front him with clarity and honesty.

In another 3-4 meetings, I could seal the deal with him. Now, how did I succeed? Was it simply by choosing to wait for my client for more than 12 hours? I could have easily left a note on his table and come back on a later date. But I didn't do that. And what happened as a result? Although the doctor had been extremely busy, he acknowledged my patience and perseverance. Also, while listening to me in his cabin, he was so impressed with my credible and compelling persuasion skill that he extended an invitation for dinner to me.

If you still associate persuasion with impishness, let me define persuasion in the simplest terms. Persuasiveness is your ability to make intentional and successful efforts in influencing someone. Persuasion is not about forcing others to come on your side. You have to nurture the art of reasoning, sharing feelings, and cleverly conveying information.

Let's say you have watched a new web series on Netflix and you tell your friends to watch the same. Will they follow you blindly and spend their precious time over a web-series? They may choose to watch it if you had been able to chalk out to them the exciting takeaways from the show in the most compelling way. Throwing a random praise over something can never make people follow your interest. Whether you are Mukesh Ambani or a guy-next-door, you can make people fall for you only with your persuasion skill.

Let me narrate another classic example. Stephen is a young MBA graduate from a not-so-famous university and he gets placed in an MNC under a boss who happens to be an MIT alumnus. The marketing team of the company is going through a tough time in identifying a good promotional strategy. Stephen has joined the team as the youngest member without the badge of a big university. However, he comes across as a confident person and has an immense knowledge of the target audience. He proposes a unique idea of influencing the market, an idea that none of his experienced team members could come up with. Initially, people raised eyebrows due to his humble background.

However, his detailed analysis of the market and the proposed strategy caught the eyes of his MIT alumnus boss. With excellent communication skill and superb emotional intelligence, he could easily make everyone in the team fall for his idea.

The Trick Of Making It More Impressive

Persuasion is a two-way road. You don't pat on the shoulder of every Tom, Dick and Harry and start persuading him to get aligned with you. Even if you do, you are just making a mockery of yourself and nothing more. You should flourish your persuasion skills only when you see the hope of success looming large.

In that Durgapur hospital, I could sense the impressiveness of its ambience. The staff was thoroughly professional and everything about the hospital seemed meticulous. I was so impressed with their system of functioning that I found it worth my while to wait for the busy doctor.

Once you are convinced that the person opposite you is worth pursuing, you have to use your communication skill to the best. Good communication skill assists in persuasion. You have to understand that your goal is to influence others to think or act in a certain way. So, how do you reach their mind? The quickest way to do that is to speak with them. While you express yourself clearly, the person opposite you is able to gauge your grip over the topic. Your vocabulary and nonverbal gestures speak a lot about your personality. Once you make your communication engaging, people are drawn to you. You have to remember that when the future is uncertain, everyone is trying to look for their best interest in your words. Let me ask you if you can persuade a hungry man to buy a smartphone?

No. Never. In fact, if you try to thrust the benefits of a smartphone to him, he will simply ask you to stop blabbering and get him a loaf of bread instead. The idea of good communication skill is to be able to reach out to the audience. You meet hundreds of people every day but rarely do they have a lasting impact on you.

The few who manage to stand out are those who impress us with their words. Have you not met at least one person in your lifetime who speaks out in public with such conviction that you feel compelled to lend your ears? Their ability to articulate their point of view and connect with the listener is tremendous. They know the power they hold and can easily impact how you think and act according to their agenda. When you can relate to someone's word, they are already asserting their influence on you. As an entrepreneur myself, I cannot stress enough the importance of speaking well to the whole bunch of youngsters who are busy nourishing the dream of entrepreneurial life. Speaking with persuasive ability is the golden key to success.

Persuasive communication is important. When you can convince people and sell your vision, you are seen as an extraordinary personality. Many strong speakers are a brand unto themselves simply because their words are their greatest selling tool. Steve Jobs delivered all his speeches in his favorite black turtleneck t-shirt and the whole bunch of budding entrepreneurs fell for his thoughts. If you watch his videos, you will be amazed to find complete absence of technical jargons or use of Tharoor like language.

But, if you are still hell-bent on equating persuasion with manipulation, then let's add a positive connotation to it. Persuasion is manipulation with the right intention. Your words should be relatable. You cannot simply try to persuade people to watch a crime drama when the audience is of Mills & Boons genre. When you speak like you understand people and their requirements, you immediately become relatable and that draws people to you in both public and personal space.

Have you seen the ongoing ad of 1mg? They have Pankaj Tripathi as the face of the brand. It has been considered a huge leap of faith in the marketing world. The actor is the face of the common man of India who understands the Indian middle-class mentality and has seen the struggles of life. If someone like him is supporting the brand of 1mg, it communicates and enhances the credibility of a brand.

Effective communication or your persuasive skill need not be a one-to-one discussion to weave a success story for you. There are countless ways to convince people and it all depends on your genuine need and intention. And that is why, your persuasion skill forms the first impression on people.

Simply put, whether you wish to convince your professor for an extra mark or you wish to propose marriage to your girlfriend or boyfriend, your success is engineered by the right approach. I would like to guide the youngsters who are on the verge of entering a career. It is often said that you have to be in the right place at the right time. Here, I would like to add that you have to be in the right place, at the right time, surrounded by the right people. You cannot sell sanitary napkins to a bunch of boys. However, you can communicate to them the significance of menstrual hygiene which they can pass on to the women in their life. All that matters is your approach towards the job you want to be done. You can have the best of the ideas and intentions, but so do countless other people. What makes you stand out in the crowd is the way you represent yourself.

For any businessman, conferences open the gate of networking. Without connecting to the right bunch of people in the market, no business can make a mark for itself as everyone in the market has a unique experience to share. But a business conference invites hundreds of experienced players for a couple of days or maybe hours. It is utterly impossible to meet each participant and inform them about your ideas and proposals. Now, whenever I attend such conferences, I carry a bunch of my business cards with me. But do I exhaust all the 15-20 cards that I carry? Absolutely not. I often check the list of the participants and single out 4-5 participants whose background and experience interest me.

Much like most of them, I too attend such meets to benefit my enterprise. So, what do I do? Do I just shake hands with them, exchange cards and ask them to join my endeavor? Ha! How I wish it was so easy and mechanized. A business is built on effective relationships. Networking doesn't happen overnight with the mere exchange of cards.

Even if you stand on the podium and share your company details and the uniqueness of your product, it is difficult to get a single deal clicked. As I spent months over building my enterprise, I realized that superficial communication with a profit-oriented mindset is not welcomed easily because every other person in the room is doing the same thing. Then where does the distinction lie for me? I take my conversation a little deeper. I never keep my words or thoughts exclusive to my business. As I delve into the interests of others in that short span of time, people tend to remember me better.

Persuading someone to look at your profile and business is not a cake walk. With so many entrepreneurs competing at the Shark Tank for funding, do you think all of them can secure investment? When you are trying to persuade someone, remember the structure of a great speech - Logos, Pathos and Ethos. Logos demands the audience's reason, building up logical arguments. Ethos reflects upon the speaker's status or authority, making the audience more likely to trust them. Pathos appeals to the emotions, trying to make the audience feel angry or sympathetic towards the information communicated. The target audience should be able to see the logic behind your persuasion. Your credibility shall matter when you are trying to convince people. So, always get your facts and figures correct when communicating with your audience. Nobody is going to buy your words unless they can really relate to what you are saying or your situation. Simply put, you cannot talk about the plight of poverty if you haven't experienced anything in that spectrum.

As an entrepreneur myself, I can tell you that success comes with an immense amount of hard work and rejection. In this era of social media, you can easily build your professional network via LinkedIn. You can follow umpteen number of people; you can leave messages for them every day and still may go unnoticed. But, instead of nagging people to show interest in you, why don't you say something that instills interest amongst people? Just drop a brochure of your newly launched product or share a video of how you work. Your focus should be on drawing beneficial attention and not an unwarranted one.

Before you boast about your power to make people queue up behind you, just ensure that you are an active listener. Understanding others' viewpoints on any given topic is crucial. You cannot persuade a Chemistry professor to teach you Creative Writing, can you? Your ability to lend your ears to others' opinions indicates at your patience meter.

You earn respect from people when they find you respectful towards them. Giving people the chance to share their thoughts makes them feel valued. This in turn helps establish trust and you are able to recognize their motivations better to prepare effective arguments to win their support. Your interpersonal skills take you a long way in this game of building relationships. In fact, if you look around and study successful people, you will find them webbed within a big network of people. The better you hone your interpersonal skills, the more efficient you will be to connect with people.

It is obvious that we need to pursue opportunities and connect with industry leaders or professionals with varying interests and perspectives to hasten growth in our career. Even if you are just entering into your college life, consciously or unconsciously, you make efforts to be in the good books of those professors who can help you in shaping your career. But, believe me, building relationships is a grueling job.

When you're sitting at your desk unsure if you would actually attend the networking event you had marked on your calendar, it's important that you muster up both the energy and the motivation to power through. As you carry the bag of your effective communication skill, channel the confidence to make authentic connections.

> "*Networking is a lot like nutrition and fitness: we know what to do, the hard part is making it a top priority.*"
> – Herminia Ibarra

Are You Emotional or Emotionally Intelligent?

When you utter your opinion, do you think that everyone in the crowd shall cheer you up for your great thoughts? You are bound to get rejections. You will be laughed at, mocked for your failed attempts to convince people. Are you emotionally prepared enough for taking such ridicule in your stride? If you feel dejected and go back into your cocoon of not-trying to let the world know about your thoughts, then you are just an emotional fool who fails to manage an emotional outburst. To be an effective persuader, you have to feed your emotional intelligence which will make you capable of managing, expressing and controlling your emotions properly. With strong emotional intelligence, you can connect with your feelings, turn ideas into action, and make sound decisions about what matters to you the most.

Furthering the same point, I wonder if we are taught enough about our emotional skills. Let's take the example of management schools. Whether it is Harvard or IIM, if you see the curriculum design, you'll find every aspect emphasizing over our analytical skills. That is, the whole world seems to be focused on our left brain. Why do we need such a hullabaloo about our analytical skills? If life were enough with our left brain, we wouldn't have got a right-brain, no? You can be an Oxford alumnus, a Nobel Laureate, however, if you fail to make emotional connections with people, not a single effort of yours can give you a fruitful outcome.

Most of the famed business leaders carry one commonality – their ability to empathize. They never carry the baggage of their aristocratic degree, position in the company or their wealth along. They carry a sense of humility towards their employees and team. Today, if Ratan Tata stands in the central hall of the Taj Mahal Hotel, everyone shall come to him without him calling out to anyone. Why? Because that's how he connects with people around. Any business is assured of failure if the leader fails to make a connection with the team. The scenario remains the same even inside a college classroom.

Would you like to attend a lecture if the professor is just dictating the notes on the topic? No. The lecture will lose its appeal even if the professor has mastery over the topic. Similarly, even if a subject is arid, students would develop interest in it if the professor is able to make an emotional connect with them.

Why do you think you have had favorite teachers in your life? For the subject or for the good looks of the teacher? Never. It is only because that teacher was able to nurture your interest in the subject by making an emotional connect with you. The next question will be how you are persuaded to choose a specific subject in your career.

A professor with whom you are emotionally connected can easily persuade you to choose a specific stream. You would agree easily because your brain knows that the professor takes care of your interest. Your right brain first ensures the emotional connect and builds the bridge of trust and then your left brain churns out the analytical skills to verify the proposition. And there lies the beauty of persuasion; it ensures taking care of the others' interests without being manipulative.

An emotionally intelligent individual is better able to manage a team and thus is an efficient persuader. When you have strengthened your emotions, you have braced yourself against the wind of change and uncertainty in life. If you are emotionally strong, you can chalk out the right communication skills to emotionally connect with other people and handle difficult conversations amicably. Better processing and understanding of emotions are the foundation of every relationship, personal or professional. If you can understand, accept, and express your own emotions better, it makes you empathetic towards others' emotions as well. Developing emotional intelligence allows you to communicate effectively and build stronger relationships. You can work on increasing emotional intelligence at any point in life. It deepens your understanding, functionality, and relationships. Let me bring to you the illusionary (mis)connections of the social networking world to make you understand the nitty-gritty of persuasion.

Let's assume that you are a creative writer who has been posting poems on the Facebook wall. You have some thousand odd connections on FB and your poems were well appreciated there. In a couple of months, you start a blog of your own and people follow your blog. However, the number of likes or appreciation did reduce a bit. A few more months pass by and you decide to publish your own book. Now, what does the author dashboard tell you? Could you sell 1000 copies? Ha!

No matter how many times you tell your never-ending FB followers to buy your book, only a handful would actually buy it. So, does that mean you are incapable of becoming a poet? No. It simply means that there is no one-size-fits-all technique about persuasion. If your emotional quotient is good enough, you'll realize that every individual bears a different taste of interests. You CANNOT persuade everyone to invest their time and money on you. You might have garnered thousands of likes on your Facebook post, but that doesn't mean all those people shall stand by your side in the time of need.

An emotional person shall be bogged down by this fact check, while an emotionally intelligent person will use this opportunity to recognize the real relationships from the fake. Emotional intelligence not only hones your persuasion skill, it also helps you to build authentic connections. Successful persuasion skills are based on your ability to have positive interactions and maintain meaningful relationships with people. In order to sustain those relationships, you must be able to work in their best interests as well.

Imagine you are trying to persuade one of your coworkers to take on a new responsibility at work. As you are talking to them, they keep their arms crossed and avoid eye contact. When they speak, their sentences are short and curt. If you are emotionally intelligent, you will be able to see that they are feeling upset or intimidated and you will be able to adjust your persuasion tactics to try to calm them down or address their concerns. The art of persuasion is an integral part of our life. From dawn to dusk, either we persuade or get persuaded.

Asking your mother to make aloo paratha for dinner or listening to the salesman in the Apple showroom – we're either convincing or getting convinced.

> *"If your emotional abilities aren't in hand, if you don't have self-awareness, if you are not able to manage your distressing emotions, if you can't have empathy and have effective relationships, then no matter how smart you are, you are not going to get very far."*
> – Daniel Goleman

Oh! Don't Be A Nagger Dagger

A few years ago, I had the opportunity of meeting the Eastern Head of one of the biggest government organizations. She was extremely tied up and could lend me only a couple of minutes to talk. It was impossible to make a mark in that time span. Nevertheless, I took the necessary contact details and kept her updated through regular mails. Months passed by and I got opportunities to attend business meets where she was one of the guests. I remember seeing people surrounding her and trying to have a word. She was always followed by aspiring businessmen and I hardly got any chance to talk to her in person. However, in a few months' time, she reached out to my office on her own to talk about a partnership.

Did I do anything extraordinary for her that made her reach out to me? All I did was to remain patient throughout. You have to understand that persuasion is like sowing a seed and you must have the patience to let that seed grow into a fruit-bearing tree. Have you watched the movie, Rocket Singh?

The protagonist is not a marketing management student. He is a simple salesman who knows the art of maintaining relationships. Your persuasion skill is required to build a healthy relationship with the other person. If you keep on nagging others to follow your path for your own benefit then believe me, it is not persuasion. It exposes your manipulative nature. Engage yourself in building and nurturing true relationships.

Out of thousands of your followers on social media networks, raise at least ten strong relationships with people whom you can call in the middle of any crisis. Let me be brutally honest here. Relationships won't build overnight. Never. People out there are not your parents or siblings; they reflect the reality of life which is nothing but a barter system. It took me years and years of hard work, patience and perseverance to build effective relationships with people. Building relationships is the art of connecting with others, aligning them with your interests and letting them bask in a win-win situation.

How do you think Paytm created its market? The Fintech was the brainchild of Vijay Shekhar Sharma who had faced failure more times than you can imagine. However, as the wrath of demonetization struck the market, he could get to the core of the common man's problem and marketed the efficacy of the digital payment at the right time. In no time, the whole country was humming the tune of *Paytm Karo*. You have to understand that building relationships is a gradual process and with patience and persistent effort, you are going to succeed. If people don't get anything good in return, they are not going to be persuaded by your words or actions.

So, next time you get a little snobbish about that gold-framed degree on your wall, please understand that a piece of paper can never make people queue behind you. Until you learn to build and value relationships, every ounce of persuasion will be thrown in the bin called nagging.

Do You Know The Person Well?

Do you know the person opposite you well? If no, then know. Without knowing a person's pulse, you can never make a move. Just tell me if you can talk about a rocket science experiment to an illiterate person or persuade a young boy to spend hours and hours listening to bhajans when his interest lies in rock music.

Persuading someone becomes easy when you know the likes and dislikes of that person. You cannot persuade people to follow an alienated route without first instilling interest about it in them. Listen to your audience, feel their needs and before you begin considering persuasion, check and recheck if your opinion would add value to their lives or not. And more than anything, empathize. You cannot make a business proposal to a client when he is attending the funeral of his mother, can you? There is a timing for everything. And believe me, there is no bigger asset than a valued relationship.

> *"Those who say "it's not personal, it's just business" are lying. All business is personal, and the best business is very personal"*
> *— Rick Lenz*

If you are at the start line of your career, you should nurture your relationship building skill more than any other expertise. Whether you have to run a team for software development or you are given a job to supervise some elderly employees, your success depends on how well you build relationships with the people under your charge. Be assured of hesitation and opposition, but once you have understood the people around you correctly, none can stop you from succeeding. Knowing someone at a personal level has its own benefits. After all, no man can be an island. We all need other people at every stage of our life. But relationships cannot be built on the basis of immediate benefits. You cannot expect immediate returns while networking with someone. The offer of help without expecting anything in return goes a long way in creating a long-term relationship.

A few years ago, I was approached by a good friend from the realty business. Over a cup of coffee, he shared his ideas with me which were unique enough to build a good business upon. I helped him in propagating those ideas without expecting anything in return. That was a goodwill gesture. That small effort of mine strengthened our bond further. After a couple of years, I had to organize a shoot for IBM.

The quotes from the 5-star hotels were unreasonably high. I turned to that friend from realty business and he helped me out for sure. The goodwill gesture shown by me in the past had borne fruit and I was able to organize the even well without losing much from my wallet.

The dawn of your career is a new canvas. Paint it with the hues of networking with the right people and there your life's canvas will become a cynosure of all time.

There will be times when any association will give an immediate good outcome. But that doesn't mean you have to ghost them as soon as the deal is over. A good pursuer builds long-term relationship. But then, considering the current scenario of pandemic, keeping in touch with people is now restricted to the virtual route. It is indeed a paradigm shift in the way we communicate. Maintaining a relationship has become a little more difficult. However, just sending a good-natured hello over WhatsApp can bring a huge difference. It makes the other person feel that it is not just a business relationship. It reflects your compassion and concern. As the pandemic situation improves, a hybrid model is making way. So, one should try and meet people in person as and when possible.

A couple of months ago, I had a conference scheduled with one of the biggest conglomerates, and there was a provision to attend the whole thing via zoom. However, I decided to participate in person. It did cost me money, time and extra effort, but that paid well. After all, there is no better way to develop connection than meeting a person in person.

Mastering The Art Of Closing Deals

When I talk about the art of persuasion, I am not just trying to preach about making human connections and understanding others' interests and all. Empathizing, active listening skills and high emotional quotient are essential for developing persuasion skill.

But, why do you need to persuade anyone in the first place? For your benefit, of course. Let's take another case of a young boy named Vikas. He has just appeared for his 12th board exam and is waiting for the result. In the meantime, instead of wasting time by doing nothing, he starts accompanying his father to their family-run saree shop in Chandni Chowk. One fine day, a young girl comes with her family to shop for her marriage and Vikas's father fails to please the customers.

Soon, Vikas applies a new strategy and displays a lehenga very similar to the one created by Manish Malhotra. He goes one step ahead by showing a picture of a celebrity who wore a similar lehenga for her engagement. That's it. The young girl is impressed with this new marketing strategy where not a single word about the technicality of lehenga making is uttered. That day, Vikas could close the deal for not only one bridal lehenga but also a few more designer sarees.

The art of persuasion is well reflected in Su-Kam's creative marketing collaterals for all its products. They used unique marketing strategies to attract customers. It was the late 90's. When every other brand tried to hire a famous celebrity, Su-Kam chose to persuade Dhaba owners around Delhi to put their dhaba name on Su-Kam board. It was a win-win situation as the dhaba owners got a board for their dhaba while the brand got its promotion. Even Kunwar Sachdev followed the same tactic on shikaras in Kashmir.

This proves that if you have great persuasion skills, you can bring anyone from any stratum of life to bring something good for you. You neither need to be the greatest of all nor you need the largest of the audience. If you wish to move ahead in life, pocket the art of humility, strong communication skill and remain proactive in your pursuit. However, there is no guarantee that you will succeed every time and your persuasion skill will work wonders.

In case you fail to persuade or crack a deal with someone, don't look at that failure as an unfathomable pit. When you opine about something, you pierce a soul which is filled with half of agony and half of hope.

All you have to do is to stir their right emotions and balance their expectations. And in this process, if your expectations turn futile, worry not. One failed persuasion is not the end of life.

> *"History has repeatedly been changed by people who had the desire and the ability to transfer their convictions and emotions to their listeners."*
> – Dale Carnegie

3

PULL YOURSELF OUT OF THE DARK PIT

Do you know that failure screams louder than your success? The most significant element in your life that invariably comes under public scrutiny is your failure. People would appreciate your glorious days, would like to have a slice from your success story, however, given a chance, they will not relent while criticizing your setbacks. Failures are inevitable. In this convoluted loop of life, you will be thrown into the darkest pit of failure where ruthless reproach will become your constant companion. But is that the end of life? Never. There will be failures that will rock your world and may alter the landscape of various relationships in your life. There will be moments when every dawn will instill a new fear and you will find yourself engulfed in confusion and uncertainty. And yet, it is OKAY to fail.

"It is impossible to live without failing at something, unless you live so cautiously that you might as well not have lived at all, in which case you have failed by default."
— J.K. Rowling

A few years ago, there was an unstoppable applause for the movie Darkest Hour for the incredible portrayal of Winston Churchill. The British Prime Minister is known for his grit and perseverance. He had a troubled childhood with negligent parents who had left him in the Harrow Boarding School even during the vacation. All his letters to his parents had gone unanswered, but he never gave up hope. One fine day, young Winston was asked to deliver a speech. He stood at the stage and simply roared a one-liner – Never, never, never Give Up!

At any point in time, if you think you are falling into a bottomless pit of failure, just look around. There will be a crevice somewhere to let some hope seep in. Failure is never final and definitely not the end of your life. It knocks at your door, lodges a bullet in your soul, only to teach you a lesson and show you a better path to success. Failure is nature's chisel that chips away all that is excess, stripping down egos as it molds and builds the right intentions. All you have to do is accept your failure and find a way to overcome it. It is said that success is all about making the right decisions at the right time. You must be present in the right place at the right time to grab the best of the opportunities. However, is it possible all the time? Success can never be by your side all the time. Without falling down, you can never understand the significance of getting up.

Failure is inescapable. Whether to drown in the pit or come out of it is entirely our choice. While the world is required to get immunized against a deadly virus, let me tell you there is no vaccine against failure. It is more like chicken pox; once you get afflicted by it, your body will be immunized automatically. Once you lick the bitter taste of failure, you can make a sweeter recipe of success. Let's say you have cracked the entrance exam for IIT but do not wish to pursue an engineering career. You wish to become an entrepreneur. You try your level best to persuade your parents to consider your choice of career, but you fail. The very next week, your parents accompany you to a counselling session and you get placed in one of the best engineering colleges in the country. What should you do now? Should you run away and pursue your dream?

You can do that, however, if you choose otherwise and give engineering a chance, you might find more students who harbor a similar mindset. You could take up some online course and learn new skills.

Incidentally, you might find your engineering curriculum helping you move closer to your entrepreneurial dream. Without making you delve too deep into the philosophy of life, let me tell you that there is nothing like missing the boat. If you happen to miss one, you can always hop into the next boat. Believe it or not, sometimes missing a boat can be a blessing in disguise. If you ever think of wailing over a missed boat, redirect your thoughts to the Titanic. Saved were those who didn't board the ship.

Break The Cocoon

Failure is a disruption. It invades our desires, hopes and aspirations. Have you ever come across anyone who wishes to fail and not succeed? Impossible. We all strive harder and harder every day only to be more successful than our peers. Whether you are a student, a software engineer or a businessman, to succeed in your endeavors is the ultimate goal. But, does it happen overnight? With life being uncertain in every aspect, failure arrives quite like an uninvited guest. You may be denied a chance to express your ideas; you may be out of job; you may end up failing in examinations; you may have a damaging breakup – Failure can enter your life in any form.

Dealing with life is a herculean task in itself. However, falling prey to failure and cutting yourself off from the world can never be a solution. It is true that criticism is always louder and sharper than appreciation. You might feel like shutting your ears and entering an impenetrable cocoon. Is that the right way to deal with failure or criticism?

It indeed feels good to be inside the bubble of safety, however, the reality is that bubbles burst far too easily. You have to understand that humans are not flawless. Each one of us, even the most successful one amongst us, carries numerous imperfections within them. Sometimes, you fail to find the deficiency in yourself and your actions, and are often bogged down when others discover them in you.

When others point out your faults, you tend to build a shield around yourself to prevent any of them invading your cozy comfort of preconceived notions. Do you think you are infallible? If yes, then you are trading with life in the most unfortunate way. Every incident, opportunity or threat, comes to you to teach you something you did not know before. A criticism knocks at your door to show where you are lacking. However, if you believe in your ideas, you should be able to embrace the naysayers and prove them wrong by flaunting an achievement. Can you prove your critics wrong by sitting inside the cocoon of failure, denial and self-pity? No. You must break that cocoon to see the world through a new lens.

"It's failure that gives you the proper perspective on success."
- Ellen DeGeneres

Let failure build a premise for hope, innovation and a better tomorrow. We have to acknowledge that the world is changing at a faster rate than ever expected. What becomes a massive hit today may become obsolete by the end of tomorrow. We are sometimes unable to match the pace at which the changes take place. If you scrutinize properly, you will find that the root cause of criticism lies in the inability to accept the changes. If you have been a top scorer throughout your academic career, you fail to accept a change in that status quo. You feel humiliated if a friend of yours beats your scores because that had never been the normal case scenario in your life.

Similarly, a renowned doctor can never believe that his child can perform poorly in academics. That becomes a prestige issue. The parents who wish to see their children getting settled into high-paying corporate jobs, fail to appreciate the idea of entrepreneurship. Every other thing that doesn't fit into our much-liked notions represents a cause of failure. Anything that challenges the status quo appears to be a miserable failure. No? Let's say you are an engineering graduate but you work as an assistant director in the film industry. No matter how much respect and money you earn at your work, you will remain a loser for that next door neighbor.

They would conclude that you had lost your mind by resigning from the software company. Every now and then, she is going to pick on your career choice in the gathering. Does that mean you should leave the work that you are passionate about? If you conduct a study of a company's workforce, you will find that 85 percent employees are unhappy with their job. They are simply working because they have to earn a living.

Apart from criticism, some dawns will wake you up with bitter and unpalatable suggestions for making peace with your failure. With my experience, I can assure you that not every suggestion is to be thrown out of the window. Some of those could be kept and brewed at a later time. Keeping yourself detached from your failure will not diminish its effects. Instead, it is better to dissect your failure to find a more innovative way to excel out of its debris. There is no harm in seeking suggestions. You are not the first one on this Earth to have failed and you will not be the last one either. You have a predecessor and will have a successor even in your path of downfall. Every failure is like a wound inflicted on your mental health and in order to heal from your failure, you have to come out of the cocoon of gloom and cultivate some better habits.

"If you can meet with triumph and disaster, and treat those two imposters just the same."
– Rudyard Kipling

In his famous poem If... Rudyard Kipling had suggested that success and failure are two sides of the same coin. In my opinion, neither of them matters enough if you wish to live a healthy and happy life. Good times vanish and so do the bad phases. Come what may, you have to pick yourself up and move on. When you fail, you are allowed to feel sad and dejected, however, the longer you take to overcome that, the deeper you go down the pit. There is no escape from feeling depressed and on the same note, there is always a way to come out that nasty feeling. Recognizing the failure is the first step you take to overcome it.

While the next step is to opt for a distraction. Regain your old hobbies, get in touch with people who understand your position well, and seek opinions from others who have seen life from your perspective. The point is, if you have won gracefully, you have to lose the same way. Inculcate the habit of accepting failure as a part and parcel of life.

Failing to clear a job interview, especially the one for which you have been working for several weeks, or failing to get a promotion or pay-rise can feel devastating at the time. But after a couple of years, when life would have moved on and brought in fresh flowers of success, all those failures would look insignificant. Those relatives who were contrasting your failure with someone's success would have forgotten it. All those people who seemed bothered by your job loss would embrace you for your present success.

A failure should not deter you from communicating with your people. When you are at your lowest, realize that there are people, family and friends, who are always there to back you. Seek support instead of grumbling inside a closed room. Share your pain with the people who understand you well at that point in life. Failure hurts and if you try to suppress your true emotions, it will be counter-productive in the long run. Just recognize your feelings for what they are and allow yourself time to feel the hurt a bit. Take a few days for the pain to lessen, then get up and get going. We feel devastated due to a failure because we had tied our identity with success. Success and failure must be perceived as mere experiences of life which do not change you as a person.

Of course, you will learn a hundred odd things while digging deep into the causes of failure, yet failure doesn't define you. Success and failure are not intrinsic parts of you. It is your patience, courage and perseverance that make you. Once you design your own vocabulary to describe success and failure, you are ready to move on. Let's say Shalini has been trying to crack the CA exam for two years. As it is considered one of the toughest exams to succeed in, everyone around accepts her failure in two attempts without offering any criticism or suggestion.

However, when she fails to clear the exam for the third time, she is heartbroken. She is going to plunge into depression when her parents ask her to look out for different options. She opens up with her parents and close friends and decides to appear for other competitive exams suitable for a commerce graduate. In no time, she lands up with a Probationary Officer position in a reputable bank. The idea of the story is to not abandon your passion, but to always keep a plan B handy. We sometimes remain focused on one door of opportunity while overlooking the other doors. Believe me, life gives us a plethora of options and it is entirely up to us if we wish to look around or not. Enrich your circle with people who will lend constructive criticism.

Lastly, while you try to cope with failure, it is important to own up a reasonable level of responsibility for your failure. Taking on too much may cause you to unnecessarily blame yourself. An exam not cleared is not the end of your life. Similarly, blaming others or unfortunate circumstances for your failure will never do any good for you. Once you accept your failure, your conscious and subconscious minds work out to find the reason for the same, and sooner or later, you are shown the mirror. If you keep blaming others for your failure, you can never rectify the mistakes you had made. When you think about your failure, you have to look for explanations and not excuses. Once you identify the reasons of your failure, you get the reign in your hands to change the outcome the next time.

> *"With a hint of good judgment, to fear nothing, not failure or suffering or even death, indicates that you value life the most. You live to the extreme; you push limits; you spend your time building legacies. Those do not die."*
> – Criss Jami

The Need For Failure

Do you know why failure is often called the stepping stone to success? Do you know failure is essential for our overall growth?

Because, no matter how much we detest it, failure leaves us with some powerful lessons of life. Experience is the first chapter in the book of failure. What happens when we fail? When we go through something, we walk away with firsthand experience. It helps us to develop a deeper understanding of life. The experience of failing at something is significant and utterly necessary because it completely alters our mindset by inflicting pain. It makes us reflect on the real nature of things and their importance in our lives, transforming and improving our future-selves.

Let me further elaborate on this concept by considering the common mistakes made by students appearing for entrance examinations. Before examinations got fit into the computer screen, OMR answer sheets were used for recording your responses to questions. All the competitive examinations share a common feature of awarding negative marks to select the cream.

Students often forget about negative marking while going through the long list of MCQs. They fail to control their urge to put to use their half-baked knowledge and keep filling the sheet. This mistake is more commonly made by the fresh candidates who then fail to clear the exams due to negative marking. However, their second attempt is always more refined and restrained. Why? Because their failure in the first attempt made them understand the mistakes they had made.

Failure adds to knowledge which can be harnessed in the future to transform that very failure into success. Nothing can replace the knowledge gained from failure. Thomas Edison is famous for having failed nearly 10,000 times before creating a commercially viable electric lightbulb. With each failure he learned what had not worked and those 10,000 accumulated failures finally paved the way to success. Failures make you resilient. The more you fail, the more irrepressible you become. Never harbor the lofty illusion that if you are good at something, you will be good at everything. Even if you are the world's best coder, not every code you write will work out well. Failure matures us. It helps us to appreciate the fine line between the right and the wrong.

We reach the deeper meanings of and understandings about life and begin to understand why we are doing the things that we're doing. This helps us to reflect and take things into perspective and derive meaning from painful situations. We live to grow and improvise ourselves to fit in the changing world. We all wish to grow and diversify to satiate our need to succeed in life. But as soon as we are knocked down by failure, we understand where we are going wrong. Failure provides us the much-needed launch pad to reach the bigger goals in our life.

We are often too worried about succeeding in life than analyzing our failures. If I shuffle through the different chapters of my life, I would say I learnt the most in life from when I failed. My failures invariably bestowed me with an unexpected zeal to do better. I was toughened for further challenges. There are some crucial elements you must churn out to come out of that pit of failure. Be courageous to think out of the box and take risks. If you are deterred by the fear of failure, will you ever be able to succeed? Failure comes to warn you about the wrong path you might be on. But with determination and persistence, you can overcome failure and move towards success. Chasing your dreams is a long journey and, in the process, there will be long years with no outcome in sight. Still, do not give up. Find an alternative to keep on moving in life. You are the best judge of your destination. If you miss one bus, it's up to you to arrange for another mode of transport. Change of transport doesn't mean you have to change your destination, does it? Failure arms you with wisdom that success often cannot.

Every biography ever written or a biopic ever made always showcases the struggles of the protagonist. Why? Because those very struggles shaped the person worth knowing. Making mistakes is good, but learning from your mistakes and not repeating them is what makes your progress. Similarly, dwelling on the past mistakes doesn't help.

Let's say, you are bitten by the bug of entrepreneurship and leave your high-paying job to start your own business. You have been good with the technical knowledge and launch an innovative app.

You however fail to market it well and hence bite the dust. Should you bury your dream of being an entrepreneur? No. You should actually find someone who holds a better knowledge of marketing. Your struggles should lead you to a fruitful solution and not towards the den of depression.

The truth is you tend to accept failure wholeheartedly only if you are doing something what you like. You should know where you wish to go and must acknowledge that the path is not going to be a bed of roses. Hurdles will come to test our creativity and will make us revise our strategy. Consider failure as that strict Physics teacher who makes you experiment with the instruments on your own to know the nitty-gritty of life. Even in a dramatically negative piece of literature, there is always a slice of optimism hidden somewhere. It could be the tenacity and persistence of the protagonist to keep going on regardless of their failure. That's where the beauty of life lies. Even if you fall in the darkest pit of depression or failure, there is always a crevice to let in a ray of light and refurbish your faith in all that is bright and joyous in life. All you have to do is to dig through the crevice. Life is bound to give us bruises and we must not hide the scars for they prove that we showed up to the challenges.

Expectations: A Burden So Onerous

It is true that the quality of our expectations often defines our actions. The more we expect from ourselves, the more we are determined to reach our target. It is often the bug of expectations that we have from ourselves that inflicts pain upon us and not so much the people or circumstances.

We all, irrespective of our age, job profile or social status, experience a constant urge to excel in whatever we do. Today, if you score 95/100 in your Mathematics paper, you try harder in the next examination to score full marks. You expect to be a better version of yourself with each passing day. Similarly, your performance in life influences others' outlook too.

People around you, your parents, friends, extended family members and even neighbors, have certain expectations from you. Every parent wants their child to do well in life. Parents strive harder and harder to make their children's life better. While doing so, they invariably end up making some unkind comparisons between their children and others. Do you remember that scene from the movie 3 Idiots where Madhavan's father was heartbroken when he received complaints about Madhavan's poor performance in engineering college? He had done everything possible to make Madhavan study well and become a top-class engineer. He couldn't digest the fact that Madhavan wished to become a wild-life photographer instead.

There prevail certain preconceived notions in our society. Any student who is academically good is forced to think about engineering or medical science as their career goals. Parents harbor some expectations from their children that often project their own unfulfilled desires. A middle-class father who works as a bank officer does not want his son to end up in the same position as his. It is not that he doesn't like his job, but he wishes his son to earn more and lead a better life that himself.

He would somehow influence his son to aspire for a better paying job. What if the son doesn't have any inclination towards that field at all? What if he wants to pursue Literature to shape his career as a writer? What if he wishes to be a tennis player but doesn't want to hurt his father's feelings and does as expected of him? In a couple of years, he may even end up in a small cubicle of a huge software company which pays him a hefty cheque at the end of the month. However, the son is never happy and keeps changing companies only to disguise his deeper discontentment.

This situation is ubiquitous. A doctor wants his son to be a more successful doctor, an Army officer fails to withstand his son's reluctance to join the armed forces, and a middle-class father fails to understand when his son leaves a big corporate house to start his own business. Expectations from ourselves and our loved ones often burden us and any diversion from the set expectations brews bitterness in the relationship.

Let's assume you are a newly married working woman. Young, dynamic, career-oriented, you are doing a great job at your work place. However, you are expected to balance your new family life along with your work life. New people, new ambience and all of a sudden you feel the burden of becoming an ideal daughter-in-law. As days pass by, you fail to bear the burden of keeping everyone happy. No matter how much you try, you seem to fall short of what the others are expecting from you.

What should you do? Should you end up your married life just because you think you are unable to balance work and family? Absolutely not. There is always a way out to solve any dispute. You have been a good negotiator at your work where your persuasion skills are always appreciated. Instead of grumbling about your new family life, you should choose to talk it out with your family members. You should lay down plainly all that you can do and communicate frankly about your expectations from the other members of the family. Once you open up about your feelings and true intentions, people who really love you will understand your predicament and start helping you out. Very soon, you'll find yourself balancing work and family beautifully.

You cannot avoid expectations from others. We are social beings and are dependent on each other. Your parents are paying for your school fees and you cannot simply ask them not to expect good result from you. When you work for a company, you are bound to follow its rules. You cannot knock at the CEO's cabin and ask him not to expect you to meet the deadlines. No. Life is a cycle of constant give and take and we can always try to make it a virtuous cycle where no one falls prey to hostile pressure. There is no escape from people and their expectations. They should however, not stop us from reaching our target.

Let me share a slice from my life here. I had a glorious career with companies like IBM and Oracle where I could win numerous awards and accolades. Even after working at a respectable position as a Solution Architect, I sensed a kind of void within me. Somehow, I was inclined towards healthcare sector from the very beginning.

It maybe because I had witnessed poor healthcare management in the remote areas of the country. So, one fine day, I left my comfortable job to start a social enterprise that provided healthcare and wellness service. Was it easy? Ha! An entrepreneur's path is strewn with prickly stones. I had to spend more than nine months running from one village to another to understand the problems and the market demand. People laughed at me and said that my decision was unsound. I was openly criticized, so much so that I was called out for my impoverished plans. People presumed my plans to be mere wanderers in the ever-growing crowd. Somehow, I knew that my vision was worth pursuing. I took every criticism with a pinch of salt, chalking out an opportunity from those challenging words. What should I call me? Braced; maybe.

But how? Am I immune to failure or depression? No. I am a human being with the same flesh and blood and emotions. When people around you see you falling short of their expectations, they take refuge in harsh criticism. It is inevitable. It is up to you if you crumble under their unfavorable comments or decide to go ahead and prove your detractors wrong. Here, I am not advocating overconfidence. Not every desire of yours shall bear fruit. If you have set your eyes clearly on your goal, you can unleash your true potential to overcome every hurdle. When people laugh at your ideas, don't take refuge into the sinkhole of emotional breakdown. Rather, reassess your target to see if it is worth pursuing. If your gut feeling says yes, then go for it.

> *"The final proof of greatness lies in being able to endure criticism without resentment."*
> – Elbert Hubbard

Whenever you feel daunted by others' expectations and criticisms, take a reality check. Who is your idol? Steve Jobs? He was thrown out of his own company once. Every successful person who has created a place of reverence in your mind has experienced upheavals in life.

If you idolize someone, put them in your place and think how they would have responded in your situation. The best way to handle any adverse situation in life is to understand the essence of criticism that you are receiving for it. Take the suggestions and overlook the tone. Come on! Not everyone can be a good communicator.

Your parents harbor good intentions for you even when they scold you or shout at you for your failed adventures. Always keep your door open to learning. If a suggestion floats by, have a quick look at it. Once you know how to improve your reality and deal with others' expectations, you become unstoppable.

When I left my prestigious job and came back home to Kharagpur, my parents were perturbed. I vividly remember the day my father and I went to Gol bazaar, a nearby market, and had met one of his friends. He had enquired about my job status and I could sense my father's hesitation. He took a thoughtful pause and then revealed that I had left my corporate job to set up my own business. The whole concept of giving up the security of a job to start a business did not align with my father's expectations from me.

The Fight Between Young And Old

Oh! The Generation Gap – A social problem that exists in every thread of our societal life. Margaret Wilson Oliphant said, "I suppose, every generation has a conceit of itself which elevates it, in its own opinion, above that which comes after it." One of the biggest problems faced by the younger generation is to make the older generation understand them.

Every generation has its own scale for measuring success and as soon the young bloods choose a different track, they are lashed out with criticism and comparison. The present situation is far worse than before because of the fast-paced life. Earlier, a difference of three decades used to divide one generation from the other but now that difference is reduced to fifteen years. Every generation faces its own set of problems and the previous generation cannot solve the issues faced by the current one.

Instead of bickering over which generation is better in handling life, it is better to find a common ground by comparing and contrasting the final results. Over the years, my father could make peace with my entrepreneurial life because I could show him the encouraging results. Having a different mindset is not a hurdle. It actually opens a window for learning something new. The generation prior to yours has certain experience that you don't have and there is no harm in learning from that.

Similarly, your generation knows more about the recent trends and market demands. If you can prove your talent in the chosen field, you can prove every criticism wrong. If your dreams are different from the lot, you have to come forward to display their power. Without demonstrating the success-failure ratio, you cannot prove your criticizers wrong. But you can never arrive at the success-failure ratio if you remain seated in that fear-of-failure den.

It is never about which generation is right or wrong; it is always about being right at the moment. There will be moments of glorious victories and damning defeats. Some will take care of your hurts while others will mock you for those setbacks. Even if you are chased by dogs in the middle of the night or fail to clear a critical job interview, there is something you can do to get over it. Hurdles do not come to end your life. You fail and you fail badly only to get up as a stronger version of yourself. All you have to do is to break the cocoon and let the ray of hope seep through.

4

FINDING A BEST FRIEND IN A STRANGER

"Saying hello doesn't have an ROI. It's about building relationships."
– Gary Veynerchuk

Humans carry an inherent desire to get acquainted with other humans. Our growth as a species revolves around our ability to connect with others. We need someone to talk to. We need someone to share our joy and understand our grief. We always need someone to lend a shoulder to lean upon. Needing someone by our side is not a sign of weakness; it makes us more humane. Let me share a funny incident from my life. I studied in Bhuvneshwar and had to go home by train. It was not a long distance from Bhuvneshwar to Kharagpur. I however, couldn't bear the bad taste of the train food. I was always unhindered in my communication. I could start a conversation with anyone without batting an eyelid or thinking twice.

My frequent journeys made me a familiar face for the pantry-car guys. They could see that I didn't like the train food at all. One day, one of those pantry-car fellows brought an omelet for me. I was surprised for I knew that egg was never in the menu.

Serving me omelet became a regular affair since then. I still remember how the other passengers used to envy on looking at my omelet. I could always sense their resentment with the special treatment I was getting.

So, was I special? Did I pay anything extra to get that special treatment? No, I didn't shell out an extra penny for the omelet. All I did was that I had built a good rapport with the person. Did I do it intentionally? Never. I just talked to the man, shared my feelings with him and let him share his with me. You may ask me if there was any need to talk to a pantry-car guy. Maybe not. I could have easily travelled every day without even looking at him. Many passengers did so and there is no harm in that too.

However, when I opened up with a simple and not a very well-to-do person, I just made him feel valued. Making someone feel valued is more important than getting any benefits in return. Not every person you interact with will be able to give you something grand in return. Not every random interaction in life is going to script a successful relationship. However, you will get plenty of chances in your life to befriend random strangers who will leave an indelible mark in your memories.

Getting a good job, climbing the ladder of success, meeting your relationship goals - you all are of course besieged by so many emotional demands at once. You don't even get time to hang out with your old friends and here I am asking you to befriend a stranger. Ridiculous! Of course, it sounds so. Moreover, you have more than a thousand connections on Facebook and you carry such a huge following on your Instagram page.

Why should you be bothered about building new relationships, that too with people whom you don't know at all? Ha! Before I accept my defeat and take back my proposal of befriending strangers, let me ask you if you have personally met all those followers. 90 percent of your so-called virtual network is restricted to the mobile screen only. It won't come forward to stand by your side in your real world.

LOSING BIG WINNING BIGGER

Let's take a case scenario. Rohit and Raju are best friends and are roommates in their Engineering college hostel. While Rohit is quite amicable in nature and doesn't differentiate between people on the basis of their looks or job profile, Raju is very picky.

He doesn't utter an extra word to people he doesn't know. Rohit talks freely to the canteen workers, housekeeping staff and everyone. He doesn't even hesitate to help those people if they need anything. Everyone in the hostel staff knows Rohit as he doesn't mind stopping for a while to talk to them. Raju and many others find Rohit going over the top. They have often labelled his behavior as stupid.

One day, Rohit falls down the hostel staircase and gets a ligament tear. Even before his friends and classmates could help him with daily chores, the hostel staff comes forward with their offer of assistance. Rohit gets all the help and support he needs from the near-strangers with whom he had just been sharing a simple hello or indulging in a casual talk.

The structure of human relationship is not built on the foundation of profit and loss. You cannot go ahead in life if you build every relationship with certain goals in mind. You cannot reserve your emotions or words for only a certain kind of people when our basic needs are multi-faceted. What if you decide to keep in touch with only those neighbors who are well-to-do or highly educated? One day, if your tap stops working, will those highly qualified people come to your rescue?

You live in a society which runs on a number of wheels and you must create a balance between all the wheels. As I said, I am quite flexible with building relationships. When I go to buy vegetables in the market, I do not carry the baggage of my wealth and achievements to the vegetable vendor. I just carry my wit along and talk to the person as a fellow human. A casual talk over trivial matters of life; a genuine query about his family's well-being – Do these things cost anything? But why should I waste those couple of minutes from my otherwise busy schedule?

Let me tell you here that one of my vegetable vendors keeps fresh green veggies separately for me. Any day, if I fail to go to the market and he has something fresh or something that I like very much, he delivers it to my house. Now, do you think I talk to him to get such benefits? No. I talk to many other vegetable vendors but not everyone comes and knocks at my door to deliver me goods.

We have to understand that not every relationship has a similar growth curve. However, getting to know someone is a simple act of living a social life. Your next-door neighbor may not be of any great use to you in your daily life, but then, do you stop saying a hello? No. Because it is basic courtesy to exchange pleasantries with people around you. That's how community life functions.

The Building Blocks Of Emotional Wellbeing

"It is very important to understand that emotional intelligence is not the opposite of Intelligence, it is not the triumph of heart over the head. It is the unique intersection of both."

– David Caruso

In current times, we are driven by technology to such an extent that we tag as 'unintelligent' all those who fail to keep pace with growing technology. We meet people online, on social media platforms and share half a dozen stories with them, but fail to open up to a person sitting next to us. We all carry with us a preconceived notion of building relationship with only those people who are intelligent. But who can define 'intelligence'?

Google can answer (almost) all your queries and probably is the most knowledgeable resource available on the Earth. It can guide you while you are choosing the best college in your field; it can help you find the best Italian restaurant in your vicinity; it can even provide you advice on dating. But when you fail in life and weep your lungs out, can Google do anything for you? That is the essential difference between machines and humans. Our ability to relate to other humans is what makes us unique. We are creatures with emotional intelligence.

We all build relationships in order to produce a conducive ambience for a wholesome life. Any healthy relationship walks a long way in extracting the best out of you. We all are strangers to each other at different walks of life before we bind together in some kind of relationship. Let's take my case of talking to the vegetable vendor.

He knows that my societal status is quite out of his league, that is, he cannot expect me to sit and have a *paan* with him. However, when I treat him well, his confidence is boosted as a human. He starts believing in the substantial role that he plays in others' lives. Let's say your housemaid is going through a financial crisis as her husband is hospitalized. Still, she comes to work lest you should deduct her salary. She doesn't seek leave fearing the same fate. And one fine day, you decide to give her a break for a couple of days and hand her some extra cash to pay medical bills. You don't expect her to return that extra money. She would surely appreciate your humanity and would come to your rescue in times of your need.

We all have our share of flaws and are constantly dealing with complex emotions. Every individual is strolling on a different plane in life and a simple smile can bridge the gap between two persons. In these fast-paced times when every day takes a new turn and unleashes a new challenge, it is often difficult to control over emotions. You may not like a particular lecturer because he looks different from the rest. You may not feel like talking to some of your classmates but unless you open up with them, you won't know their value as individuals. While this virtual world is slowly creeping inside our life, we are losing touch with the real world, and that is a huge deterrent to our growth. Why do you think schools and colleges encourage teamwork?

The projects are handed over to a team to help the members understand the importance of building relationships. Different heads generate different kinds of ideas and every member of the team learns from each other. There will be conflict in ideologies, but as you start valuing the bond amongst the team members, you will learn the process of conflict management. Once you hone the skill of bridging the gaps and building relationships, you have learnt a vital lesson in your professional life.

The essence of emotional wellbeing lies in your ability to maintain and nurture your relationships with people around you. You never know when you might need the other person. The real life doesn't depend on how many likes you gather on Facebook post.

It is sprinkled with hurdles and challenges on a daily basis and there is no one person who can solve all the problems. You can have a wonderful relationship with your boss but he won't come to repair your leaking tap. Will he? When life is strange, it is better to befriend a stranger. Have you ever wondered why passengers on a flight hardly ever talk to each other, while people travelling by train often open up with their co-passengers? People befriend strangers in a train journey for it is going to be long with nothing more to do than talking to each other. However, a flight is more often a matter of a couple of hours and people do not see the need of building any connection with anyone around. Quite like a train journey, life is long with different stations to stop by. Every passenger on this journey has their own story to tell. While we detest some stories, some others stay close to our heart forever.

In the midst of constant struggle to excel in life, our interaction with other humans helps in bringing some peace to our mind. As and when we add blocks to build relationship, we kindle trust in our heart. No person can live in isolation. Whether you are a student, a working professional or the CEO of a company, you need company of other people. When you start trusting people around you, you begin to de-stress your mind and perform better in every aspect of life. Let's say you have been recruited in a company through the campus placement. You are just 24 years old, a fresh graduate and do not know much about the corporate lifestyle. On the first day of your office, you are shown your small cubicle and your supervisor gives you a job to finish. You find your office ambience eerily different. Every head is focused on their own laptop screen with no words uttered. The walls are bouncing back only the keyboard clatter. At 12.30, the lunch bell rings and some remain boxed inside their cubicle with their tiffin box and a few go to the canteen. By the end of the day, you finish your work and go back home.

You feel weird about the working condition but somehow console your mind by considering it the first-day-at-work syndrome. However, the situation doesn't alter even after a month and you decide to quit.

Why? Did you not like your job? You were paid well with a good number of fringe benefits but still you left because people cannot usually work without building any relationships. In just one month, you must have feared that you were becoming more of a machine, devoid of any emotions, simply producing a desirable output. Your emotional wellbeing had come under threat even though there was no extra burden of work. Dearth of human interaction and unfriendly ambience made you leave the job.

Let's take another case scenario. You are a fresh graduate and have got placed in a renowned MNC. You are nervous of being a part of such a huge conglomerate. As you stand before the office building, you can feel your forehead drenched with sweat. You feel numb in your legs fearing about your colleagues' reactions to you. Will they laugh at you? Will they bully you? Your mind is getting cluttered with all sorts of murky thoughts. And then, all of a sudden, a middle-aged lady taps on your shoulder. She is the same lady who was there on that recruitment team. She calls you by your name in a friendly manner. She enquires about your wellbeing, your family while taking you inside the office building. You are given a warm welcome by a big group of people at your new office. You are introduced to your team and everyone in the team makes it a point to make you comfortable. Within a week's time, you befriend many of your colleagues and start liking your job. Those once-upon-a-time strangers have now become your go-to persons. In a couple of months, you can see an improvement is your performance at work and you are now a more confident version of yourself.

When you meet different people from different backgrounds, you diversify your experience. Every random person carries a plethora of information and experience and every time you talk to them, you learn something totally new. Befriending someone is not a rocket science. A few crucial behavioral changes and you can befriend anyone in life. One of the crucial requirements is having a positive attitude. It is the key to a successful and healthy relationship. If you keep looking at the negative side of an individual, you are simply watering a barren land.

You need not check out the educational qualifications of your chimney cleaner or how good he looks. A casual talk with him will make him comfortable while working for you. Similarly, if you are working in a team, your goal is to complete the given project while coordinating with each other. You have to focus on the efficiency of your partners and not on other aspects. If you are in a relationship, you should focus more on the positive attributes of your partner. No one is flawless, but if you keep pointing out the blemishes, you are definitely missing out on the beauty of life. Once you learn to appreciate people, your social life improves. When you appreciate others for their success or efforts, you help them feel happy and in turn boost your happy hormones too.

You can only befriend someone by talking to them. Effective communication is one of the major factors contributing to a healthy relationship among people. The language you use, the way you speak, matters a lot while talking to strangers. Your humility can take you a long way for no one in this mortal world likes to be treated lightly. As you carry your asset of effective communication, do not forget to be a patient listener. Always listen to what the other person has to say.

Never underestimate anyone. You never know when someone can come up with a brilliant idea. Moreover, you have to learn to count your words. Be careful of what you say for you never know when your words would touch the wrong nerve of the other person. One needs to communicate effectively for successful relationships. The other person must understand what you intend to communicate. Remember that you need to choose your words correctly and the message must be clear. Don't keep the other person in confusion. Transparency is the key to any relationship. On the same note, we should know where to draw the line.

Being friends with someone does not mean that you need to reveal all your secrets and disclose confidential information. When you initiate a relationship with a stranger, you invest your emotions into the other person. Relationships are demanding. You need to give your time.

You cannot just propose someone on Valentine's Day and push off. Every relationship matures over time for time reveals the true colors of a person. Time is one of the most important factors which decides the fate of any relationship, be it in college, office or personal space. You need to give time to your peers and people around you. Lending a sympathetic ear to others' problems is one of the best qualities you can cultivate. Talking to people and wishing them well is not equivalent to poking your nose inside their private lives. Wish them on their birthdays, wave a Hi when you cross them on the road, spare a couple of minutes and enquire about their life – such small gestures go a long way in breaking the ice and strengthening the bond.

Believe me, it doesn't cost much to take your eyes off the mobile screen and share a laugh with someone. When you keep scrolling down your smartphone like a rosary, you are invariably missing the essence of real life around you.

Is Social Media The Answer?

> *"Social media is training us to compare our lives instead of appreciating everything we are. No wonder why everyone is always depressed."*
> – Bill Murray

Somehow, human feelings have got metamorphosed into mere status update. Without an iota of doubt, I can tell that our lives are influenced by the number of likes on a Facebook post or number of followers on Insta-handle. What is the first thing that crosses your mind when you hear about finding a friend in a stranger?

I am sure you will be prompt to justify the statement with your innumerable friends on the social media sites. Social media has been a boon for our networking abilities as it has brought in the concept of getting connected to people on a virtual platform. A few decades earlier, students shifting to a foreign land found it difficult to go to a place without knowing anyone at all. However, the scenario is completely different in the present times.

There are several groups on Facebook where you can get in touch with people belonging to your chosen foreign university. You can get in touch with Indian communities living in a foreign country and can befriend them to seek help in relocating.

Whether you are looking for a change of job or trying to promote your book, blog or business, social networking sites have invariably become our only answer. Moreover, during the pandemic, as the world shut down completely, this virtual world became our go-to place. We could sit in the comfort of our homes and order food, vegetables, medicines and every other essential item. The schools and colleges ran on the small screen of our mobile phones and there we could keep in touch with everyone around us.

Even in my profession, I could see how strangers found it easier to connect with me and my team to seek medical help. With everything coming under the control of just one click over the internet, life seems to have become easier than ever. But, don't you feel as if you are losing touch with reality? Don't you realize that you are so enamored by the virtual world that you fail to connect with people in the real world? As everything glitters over the virtual platforms, our over-indulgence with social media is cutting us off from the reality of life. In our zeal to show off and be better than the others, we have blissfully forgotten to be kind and empathetic to others.

Our complete world has undergone an unfortunate paradigm shift. Our reliance on social media to develop personal and professional relationships has robbed us of many inter-personal skills as social animals. Far from the world of web, we humans are supposed to make real connections with fellow humans by employing our basic human skills such as communication, persuasion, kindness, patience and humility. The human aspect of our existence is fading behind the random clicks over the internet.

Sometimes, it is as if we all are hastily vacating this world of reality only to inhabit a world where everyone looks amazingly beautiful through beauty apps, appears affluent through forged information and what not.

Today, a great number of human relationships have been transferred from personal encounters to online chats. You are more comfortable talking to a person with a profile picture of Angelina Jolie than talking to someone working next to you. Instead of going to the ice-cream shop in the next lane, you prefer to order your favorite ice-cream online even if it requires you to pay extra for the delivery charges.

There is hardly any human activity that cannot be accomplished without the physical presence of the parties involved. From e-commerce to online dating, everything has made its way to the virtual platform. Whether this transformation is for better or for worse is not so much the issue as is the fact that we have built a world we can no longer do without. A surrogate culture has settled in to take the place of traditional human way of life. We are feeding a culture where technology acts as the improviser for humans. We all have reached a stage where we relate more to the technical world than to the fellow humans. Coming to think of it, our daily life is now shackled with technological bureaucracies, so much so that, we all fail to initiate a human connection in the real world.

Let's look at this hypothetical incident. You are in your mid-20s and are actively looking for a companion. All your friends in college have girlfriends or boyfriends and you are feeling left out in the gathering. You create an account on an online dating site and get in touch with a girl. Over a period of 6 months, you both interact with each other while spending long hours over the internet and also over the phone. Her voice is mellifluous and she looks out of the world in her profile picture. After some time, you really feel attached to her and decide to meet her in person. She sounds hesitant and avoids the proposal of meeting you in person. You give her some more time to know you better and, in the meantime, have woven a dream of spending the rest of your life with her. One fine day, after your constant persuasion, she agrees to meet you in person in a café.

You both decide on a dress code and a particular table to identify each other. You reach the meeting place before the decided time as a weird thought keeps occurring to you.

There is a slight mistrust in your head as she had been hesitant towards meeting you in person. Is she different from what she looks in the profile picture? You go through all your chats all over again. You run your eyes through her social media profiles again and again to find out if you had missed out on anything. And there she comes and looks out for you while you are struggling with your doubts. She looks the same as in the picture, only a little shorter. That's alright, for you have fallen in love with the way she talks, giggles and utters her buzz words. All your doubts vanish but as you are about to come out from your hiding, you find her limping.

What! She never told anything about limping. You remain hidden and start checking her pictures on Facebook. Nowhere has she seemed to have a limp. Something whispers in your ears to check on her videos. Oh! She had never posted any videos. Your dream girl limps? What will your friends think about you? You feel like escaping from the place but she sees you. You wave at her and try to initiate a normal conversation but there remains a hint of dismay on your face. Somehow, every ounce of her beautiful face and mellifluous voice fades away with that limp.

In that short span of time, your heart struggles but your mind says no to go ahead with the relationship. You start acting out weird and your impatience comes out bare. She too senses your discomfort as you keep glancing at her leg and indirectly blame her for hiding this fact. Drenched with unkindness, your sharp words pierce through her emotions and she decides to leave the place. You too do not try to stop her for you feel cheated. You had invested your emotions for almost a year into that relationship, how could it be so easy to come out of it?

Over a couple of weeks, you fall prey to depression. You could neither move ahead in life nor digest the facts. She, on the other hand, makes it clear that she was never asked about any deformities. She tags you as unkind and prejudiced with a myopic view of life. In short, both she and you go through an unbearable emotional turmoil. Now, why did things take such a bitter turn? The answer goes back to the root of virtual world.

The relationship was mediated by software, hardware and other computer mechanism, so much so that your comfort zone was actually in the virtual world. While you spoke over the phone or through chat rooms, your consciousness resided with the picture you were seeing on the screen. You never let your relationship thrive in the world of flesh and blood. You were so engrossed in those pictures on the internet that you had lost connection with the real world. It would not be difficult to refute this experience with a contrary story, as many friendships that begin on the internet, do prosper in person as well. However, failed relationships outnumber the successful ones as the internet provides a medium where people can portray themselves differently from what they actually are. It's easier to lie about one's achievements or physical capabilities on the internet than in person.

Befriending a stranger is our inherent skill. We can never thrive in an island with no one to talk to or socialize with. If you are aware of Maslow's hierarchy of needs, you will realize how every need of a human being is directly or indirectly fulfilled by another human. On the same note, as our psychology is shifting towards making connections in the virtual world, we are losing our ability to thrive in the real world.

> *"The screen is a window through which one sees a virtual world. The challenge is to make that world look real, act real, sound real, feel real."*
> — Ivan Sutherland

Are We Losing Out On Reality?

Has it ever happened to that you are driving through an unknown alley and GPS madam guides you to the destination, but you end up in the middle of nowhere? You fail to find the address and GPS madam keeps screaming that You are lost. This is a common scenario in a country like India where every alternate lane can have a shop with the same name. GPS fails. But tell me if we didn't live before the advent of Google or GPS. Of course, we did.

We used to get out of the car, go to the nearby tea shop and ask for the address. These people have always been the unpaid and unadmired version of our GPS. There was a time when we used to stop by the tea shop to enquire about an address and ended up having a hot cup of tea with some delicious non-branded cookies.

Have we not lost that beauty of life in the present time? The beauty of real life actually resides in its limitations. It may not answer all your queries like Google does, but it does help in building relationships. According to the psychological studies, one of the greatest challenges for people in the near future will be to feel comfortable in the world of reality. Giving up the convenience of virtual communication and its breathtaking speed, how many of you are willing to travel the long distance necessary to visit a friend? All we ever need to do is to just dial some digits or type a message on WhatsApp to be connected immediately.

This urge to get everything done immediately, without putting an extra effort, has landed us in a world that is utterly disconnected. There is a dearth of physical intimacy in virtual world. Let's say, you are travelling by bus and your neighbor on the next seat wishes to talk with you about the book you are holding. However, seeing you completely engrossed in your mobile phone, he hesitates to intrude. He is anyways a stranger, what value could he have added to your life? But then, what value is added to your life while you simply scroll down the Facebook page? We are invariably becoming more isolated and estranged due to our reliance on our technical devices.

If you think for a while, that stranger, who was interested in your book, could have talked about that particular author or about other books of the similar genre. You both could have actually gained some knowledge by having a casual talk. This habit of detaching ourselves from the real world is leading us to loneliness. Investing time and energy in the virtual world may keep you occupied. But in this process, you lose out on communication skills and your ability to empathize with others. Typing a comment on a Facebook post is different from starting a real-life conversation.

Do you realize that our inclination towards this virtual world has hardened us a great deal? When I ask you to befriend a stranger, I am sure you must be feeling awkward. How can you start a conversation in the middle of nowhere? Let's say, you are travelling by a public transport and you are surrounded by a number of strangers. Whom do you choose to start a conversation with? You get a vacant seat to sit in and your neighbor just take a glance at you. Just say a casual hello. It won't snatch anything away from you. The key to start a conversation is to begin at the first encounter itself. Think about it. Can you start a conversation after fifteen minutes have passed by? No.

Giving time to start a conversation opens the door to awkwardness. What would happen if you smile at and greet your co-passenger? He/she will be perplexed for a moment and then will respond with either a smile or a hello. What are the probabilities of continuing the conversation? Either zero or 100 per cent. Your co-passenger could put on the headphone, which is a gesture of being disinterested, or could show interest by adding a query. Believe me, there are more chances for the latter as all of us are looking for real connections.

You can always lower the strangers' guard by sharing a personal story with them. No, I am not asking you to share your bank details with the stranger. It is about making personal connections via something that is common between all. You can comment on the weather or talk about your destination. Whether it is a mutual friend, location, experience, or point of view, find something in common with another person and start a conversation.

While the weather is always a safe topic, you can also ask the person if they have children or pets. Similarly, now a days, we are used to seeing people walking down a hall with their head down or sitting at a table engrossed with their phone. Your body language speaks volumes. Instead of showing interest in the virtual world, try to show interest in people around. You need not become an extrovert to talk to a stranger. We often feel shy and hesitant because we are more worried about what the other person is going to think.

Believe me, everyone around you is sailing in the same boat and expecting the other person to break the ice. Are you a good listener? If you are one, then you are sure to benefit with any kind of relationship you build with the strangers. We often think that to win people over, we have to be impressive by talking something interesting. We often hesitate to initiate any conversation for lack of confidence. What if you apply a new strategy altogether? Start a conversation with strangers considering them to be more impressive than you are. People like talking about themselves, it's just a fact. So, focus on other people and genuinely listen to what they have to say. Come up with thoughtful, open-ended questions instead of making small, boring monotonous talks.

> *"A good friend is a connection to life - a tie to the past, a road to the future, the key to sanity in a totally insane world."*
> – Lois Wyse

The core idea behind befriending a stranger is to nurture our ability to talk to people without expecting anything in return. It is about honing our communication skill, building a network of people outside the realms of the virtual world in order to enhance our appeal as a person. We are not machines. In our pursuit to build followers on a social media platform, we must not forget the ground reality of our existence. Behind the façade of social media, there lies a beautiful human life where things are real, emotions are real. Once you break the ice with a stranger, you unlock the door to new knowledge and experiences which help you grow in life.

5

A SALARY OF IDLI – VADA

"The goal of mankind is knowledge. What man learns is really what he discovers by taking the cover off his own soul, which is a mine of infinite knowledge."
– Swami Vivekananda

Even though the younger generation goes gaga over the success stories of Mark Zuckerberg or Jack Ma, Swami Vivekananda remains one of the greatest inspirations of youth. The Hindu spiritual leader and Indian reformer who took Indian spirituality to the western world of materialism walked a life worthier than many successful entrepreneurs of these days. Born as Narendranath Datta in an upper-middle-class family, his pre-monastic life changed dramatically after meeting Ramakrishna. Naren's father was a lawyer and had a substantial income. His expenditure however, surpassed his earning.

It was February of 1884 and Naren was preparing for his upcoming F.A. examinations. His father's untimely death had left the family bankrupt. Creditors kept demanding the repayment of loans, and relatives threatened to remove the family from their ancestral home. Naren, once the son of a well-to-do family, became one of the poorest students in his college. He had to take up the responsibility of his family and he often failed to fulfil their basic needs.

Narendranath became acquainted with the 19th-century mystic saint Ramakrishna in 1881 and used to visit Dakshineswar just to pay a visit to Ramakrishna. In that difficult phase, his visits to Dakshineswar increased in number, and he found solace in the company of Ramakrishna. One day, Naren requested Ramakrishna to pray to Goddess Kali, the Divine Mother, for sending some financial aid to his family. Ramakrishna instructed him to go to the idol and ask for money. Naren went inside the temple thrice. Each time he could ask only for knowledge and more knowledge. Every time he came out, he confessed that he forgot about the financial needs of the family and could never ask for anything apart from knowledge.

What kind of absurdity? If you have financial needs, you need to acquire money and not knowledge. Knowledge cannot put food on your plate or get you a new mobile phone. Moreover, it is the 21st century, who cares about knowledge? It is all about making money, by hook or by crook. If you desire for luxuries and comfort, you have to trade your life for acquiring money and nothing else. There is no bigger lie than saying that money cannot buy happiness. Once you lounge in the midst of all the comforts of life, you realize the significance of money. What is the use of a degree if it cannot feed you or let you enjoy the luxuries of life? I am sure, all of you will approve of these lines in chorus. Money IS important, and it is indeed needed to fulfill our physical, physiological and emotional needs. However, are you born holding a box full of gold coins or something? Of course, there are people who are born with a silver spoon and inherit all kinds of luxuries right from their birth.

As an example, Isha Ambani, Anant Ambani and Akash Ambani are indeed born in the midst of the world's best luxuries of life. But do they sleep over all the wealth they have inherited? No. Money is important and a necessity. Money being one of the biggest necessities of human life, we all have to strive harder to earn it.

There is no harm in amassing wealth. However, nobody can gather wealth without keeping a firm grip over knowledge. As you prepare yourself to step into adulthood, you are allowed to dream of a life full of luxuries – a big bungalow or a sea-facing flat in one of the posh localities, luxury cars, prestigious jobs and everything that glitters in the material world. But the question remains how you are going to get all those.

Make Knowledge Your Weapon

"Your money can be inflated away but your knowledge and talent cannot."
– Warren Buffet

Can you imagine getting your engineering degree or MBA certificate without learning ABCD? If earning money is the ultimate motive in your life, you cannot escape from climbing the ladder of knowledge.

You have to learn the functions of gear, accelerator and brake before you start driving on the road. Money can get you a car, but you cannot drive it without learning the nitty-gritty of driving. We have come a long way by virtue of our curiosity. We kept gathering knowledge from every corner of the world and have transformed ourselves into the most intelligent living being. Knowledge has always been our weapon to succeed in life. Be it the discovery of antibiotics or developing cellular phones, knowledge has been the key to success, power, and respect.

Do you get a job because you have a million dollars stored in your locker? No. You may ask if someone has a million dollars in their locker, why would they even look for a job. Ha! Much like humans, money is a mortal matter.

Money is exhaustible. Your coffers are going to be empty someday if you fail to keep filling them. On the same note, you do not wake up with money stuffed under your pillow. You have to work to earn money and to work, you have to have some knowledge. There lies a curious case with knowledge. With too much knowledge, you draw in unwarranted competition and make enemies, while with too little, you drown in the pit of failure. However, once you find the right balance, you churn out your own recipe of success.

Being born in the town of Kharagpur, I was lucky enough to be surrounded by the glow of IITians. I was quite young and not a student of IIT Kharagpur. I was not allowed in their library but I carried an unquenchable thirst to get some books. I used to approach the librarian and he would simply throw me out for I didn't have any pass to use the books. I became adamant and I didn't give up. Every now and then, I used to knock at his door to get hold of some books. In a couple of weeks, my persistence was acknowledged and I was allowed to borrow a few books. You have to understand that your success story can be scripted by only your determination.

There are indeed different elements to your success, be it knowledge, experience or money. However, you can be successful when you are determined to run the virtuous cycle of upskilling your knowledge. I was in my 11th standard when I had learned Windows Programming which was not a part of my academic syllabus. None of my friends were learning that. No other school going children took a sneak-peek into IIT library. Then, what was my special need to acquire so much knowledge?

I was not going to get extra marks for my programming skills. That librarian wouldn't have given me a job for repeatedly knocking at his door. Then why? Knowledge has always been my weapon to conquer success. When I was doing that Windows Programming, I was not thinking of earning an extra mark or money. Most of the times, acquiring knowledge is done for the sheer pleasure of discovering something unknown. I was so carried away by the number of books lined up in that library that I befriended that librarian.

He was a stranger to me and yet he could see my determination for gaining knowledge and finally allowed me to take some books. If success is equivalent to earning money, then gaining knowledge is your first step in that chase.

Right now, you are bestowed with several options to choose from. Even if you have been a science student, you can switch to management courses for they seem to equip you for more lucrative jobs. Don't we see engineering graduates aspiring to join the prestigious IIMs? It's common to diversify when all you want is to earn a good living. However, no one can diversify without building a strong foundation of knowledge. You cannot chair the finance department of an MNC without understanding the basics of accounting. Even if you dream of being an entrepreneur and have come up with a brilliant idea, you will need some knowledge to propagate the idea in the market. Whether you are queuing up for seeking admission to one of the best colleges or you are beginning at a new job, your growth will be influenced by competition. And believe me, this idea of competing is going to remain your constant companion at every stage of your life. Your ability to outperform others lies in your diverse knowledge domain.

Let me craft a hypothetical case scenario here. Shalini is a fresh engineering graduate and instead of applying for a job, she wishes to pursue a higher degree from one of the most prestigious universities in the US. She is all set to move, but then the whole world falls prey to a complete lockdown. Though her admission status remains intact, she fails to cross the borders. Two months pass by and the academic year doesn't start. Instead of wasting time, she utilizes her literary skills by starting a blog. She keeps posting articles after articles, and one fine day, she is spotted and is invited to become a guest columnist in a well-known magazine. How can an engineer become a columnist and that too in the non-technology section? Her deep interest in literature was not for any particular professional benefit. She had just been a voracious reader and over the years, she could run her ink well. She takes up the part-time job and learns the business of publishing.

In a few months' time, as the academic calendar starts, she switches back to her desired course. Her free time indulgence however, added a feather to her resume. Now, if at any time she wishes to put to use her writing skills, she knows whom to approach and how to proceed.

Widening your spectrum of knowledge can never be a waste of time. Sometimes, you may end up earning not a single penny but you will certainly earn something that others don't have. Diversifying your skills makes an enormous positive impact on different aspects of your life, be it academic or professional. Whenever we challenge ourselves with a realm untouched, we expand our horizons. You may be at any stage of life, there is always a room for improvement. In a world of constant change, staying stagnant is of no use. Without building on the edifice of your knowledge, you halt your progress.

> *"The key to pursuing excellence is to embrace an organic, long-term learning process, and not to live in a shell of static, safe mediocrity. Usually, growth comes at the expense of previous comfort or safety."*
> — Josh Waitzkin

Specializations Come With An Expiry Date

There is no denying that every young blood is dying to do a specialization. As the world twirls around technology, apps and gadgets, every second guy in the crowd wants to become a software engineer. You work hard, study almost 18 hours a day and get a glorious engineering degree. As soon as you finish your course, the market scenario changes and you don't get placed like the way you wanted. Sooner or later, you realize that a specialist can of course enjoy a short-term gain but specialization is never sufficient for your long-term goal.

I have realized this in my own career. I was working in NRSA, Hyderabad, as a junior scientist. Being a government office, the lab used to be closed by 5 pm in the evening. On my way back home, I used to cross a small setting of graphic designing.

Somehow, I was fascinated by this whole new concept of graphic designing due to my inherent liking towards comic books. One evening, I approached the shop (that's what it looked like) and asked them to teach me graphic designing.

They turned down my request as they were not there to teach anyone. They had their clients for whom their team used to design. So, I rephrased my question to them and asked them to employ me. The man looked annoyed and curtly refused me for there was no vacancy. Since then, every second evening I used to knock at their door asking for work. Why? I had a good job; then why should I be worried about working on something which I had never learned?

The answer lay in my interest in diversifying. I wanted to do something which I hadn't done before. And believe me, seeing my persistent efforts, this graphic designing place allowed me to work with their team in exchange for food. My salary was Idli-Vada. Hilarious, no? In that small setting, while I learned the basics of graphic designing through practical exposure, I could get a closer look at how a business is run. Never did I know that one day I would be running a company of my own with my own set of clients.

Learning something new is an asset in itself. Whether you are in school, or college, or starting your career, you are going to be challenged by the uncertainties of life. Anything learned accidentally or intentionally with no immediate use in the present can become your savior at the time of crisis.

When starting your career, your specialization can command a higher return for your hard-won skills. However, as years pass by, you will realize that your audience is reducing in size. Without a wider range of competencies, you will often have trouble seeing the forest for the trees. Let's say, you are very good with your molecular biology skills and get placed in one of the reputed research labs in the country to pursue your doctorate degree. Five years of consistent efforts and you have made some remarkable propositions in your thesis.

However, you have been a bad communicator with poor speaking skills. Then how would you present your work in front of the thesis committee? You had always thought that your specialization in molecular biology would be enough for you to excel in the world of science. But then, if you cannot present your achievements, how can you excel in the field?

Before you make a hue and cry over any specialization, do realize that specialization often comes with an expiry date. Very soon, the specialist's skills are no longer the hot new skills or methods, something else can come along to displace it. Remember how Nokia phones were thrown out of the market? If you fail to diversify or learn a new skill, you are just saturating yourself and heading towards a dead end.

But then, if specialization is such a bad thing, why do universities provide specialist courses or job market advertes for specialist job profiles? Specialization is not bad at all. It is that diversification and constant learning are the added assets that one should keep gathering. The more you diversify, the more skills you attain, and in turn, you become more productive and dynamic.

When you widen your knowledge base and learn a new skill, you hedge against one skill becoming obsolete. Learning something new also allows higher level thinking where you open the door to a different perspective. The more you learn, the more value you add to your overall life, and that too on a long-term basis. That small shop of graphic designing had given me only Idli-Vada in exchange for my working hours but my eyes were opened towards the pros and cons of running a business. On top of it, when I work with any graphic designing team for my own company, I don't stare at their offerings like a fool. I can deal with them knowingly for I understand how the whole graphic designing thing works. As Peter Drucker said, *"The only skill that will be important in the 21st century is the skill of learning new skills. Everything else will become obsolete over time."*

Learn Till You Die

Recently, the web series called Rocket Boys gained a lot of popularity. Based on the lives of Homi Bhabha, Vikram Sarabhai and Abdul Kalam, the series is based on the incidents displaying their hardwork and persistence to bring India on the global platform of Science. While Sarabhai and Bhabha came from an affluent background, Kalam scripted his success story through perseverance.

He came from a humble background and none of his family members was educated. He was always known as a hardworking and bright student in school. He used to study from 7-8 PM till 11 PM under the light of a kerosene lamp as electricity had not reached his town in those days. His mother used to keep kerosene for his study at night. Kalam was a firm believer in the power of knowledge. It must not have been easy for someone to cover such vast expanses of knowledge coming from a family of near illiterates. However, Kalam never hesitated to learn something new or walk into an aisle that had not been walked in before.

> *"The purpose of education is to make good human beings with skill and expertise. Enlightened human beings can be created by teachers."*
> – A.P.J. Abdul Kalam

There is a famous Chinese proverb that urges one to keep learning till the day one dies. The saying holds significance for its insistence on the need to upskilling ourselves. As a fresh graduate, you may feel that you have learned enough to earn a handsome salary. You get placed in a reputed company and start working in a position you always wanted to be in. As there is no complaint towards your performance, you remain cushioned inside that comfort zone and never think of upskilling yourself. A couple of years pass by and soon you realize that people who had joined after you have diversified their skills and have moved on to a higher level.

At that point in time, that comforting cushion starts pricking you as you have lost some golden opportunities in life by just being stagnant. Now, the question is how far you should go in diversifying yourself?

I shall give my example here. I am not a person from Finance background, but for running a company like iKure, I cannot be blindfolded by any random finance guy. I need not know every section of Business law or the details of accounting, but I do know the basics so that in a board meeting with my finance department, I do not sound like an ignorant person.

Sometimes, ignorance is bliss. You need not know what is going on in your neighbor's house, but you can no longer remain ignorant to different skills that can help you grow in your life and get your job done. Let us think about the prevailing pandemic situation. You need not know the procedures involved in treating Covid patients, but you cannot remain ignorant about the symptoms of the disease. Can you?

You need not queue up for getting a medical degree to apply your common sense. When life is uncertain and is bound to throw new challenges every now and then, you have to be flexible to go beyond your formal education. You can become a biotechnologist and play around genes and cloning techniques, but you still need to acquire basic computer knowledge. You need not know coding or programming, but you cannot run away from learning the basic applications like MS Office.

When you leave the hallowed grounds of formal education, you have to face a world full of new challenges. Bookish knowledge brings you benefits but you cannot survive in the world unless you acquire practical knowledge as well. For example, when I decided to learn graphic designing, I could have easily got enrolled in a proper training institute. I could have asked my father to give me some money, instead of banging my head everyday at that shop and receiving Idli-Vada as salary. Then why didn't I do that? Just imagine a case scenario where I take admission in a proper institute to learn graphic designing. The institute has a well-qualified teacher, and in a couple of months, he makes me well-versed in graphic designing. When I come out of the institute, I get a certificate in hand for my graphic designing skills. But I have zero knowledge about how to handle clients, what kind of demands there are in the market and how to market my skills in the world full of qualified people.

Educating yourself to receive a degree is only one facet of learning. Though formal education is important, because no one is going to give you a software engineer's job if you do not have the basic engineering degree, you have to understand that no job profile fits exactly into your educational profile.

For example, software engineering books will not teach you interpersonal skills or how to handle a difficult situation in the office. You have to learn that from other sources. Let me share a slice from my life with you. When I was inducted into IBM, I was introduced as a performance engineering expert. I still remember that I was taken aback by my job profile in front of 20-25 people in a conference room. I didn't even know what performance engineering was and my supervisor had happily introduced me as an expert in that field. Now, I could have simply said no to the assigned job, but I chose otherwise. Of course, I had to work for 16 hours a day to learn the skills required for the job profile, which would have been difficult for anyone. I could have easily given up, but learning something new was always my core objective.

When you progress on the path of gaining knowledge, you cannot rely on some stringent rules. If you want to widen your knowledge domain, you have to carry a token of flexibility in your purse. Let us consider an imaginary situation where you have to reach a place and all of a sudden, your flight gets cancelled when you are at the airport. You have never travelled by train as your parents are well off, but now you have no choice but to travel by train if you wish to reach your destination.

There are two options open to you - either you drop the whole plan of travelling and reschedule it to another convenient date, or you can throw all your inhibitions to the wind and travel by train. The second option offers you a chance to do something that you have never done before. You may definitely face some trouble in the beginning, but the learning from that experience will be very valuable. Due to improved standards of living, the present generation enjoys almost all comforts of life right from the beginning of their life.

When comforts are available to you without much efforts on your part, you tend to forget the concept of hardwork, persistence and perseverance. You invariably keep demanding for more and more. Let us take the same example of train travel. What if you fail to get a confirmed ticket?

You have never traveled by train, then how are you going to travel in a severely cramped general compartment? If you prioritize your journey, you will never fear traveling by any means. A young mind needs to be free from all shackles of unnecessary comfort and should be welcoming every kind of new experience that broadens their knowledge of life. Becoming flexible is not about compromising on your basic needs or comfort. Flexibility is about open-mindedness. Once you finish your college life, you will of course opt for a stable job that suits your educational profile and interests. Initially, your job profile will look alluring, but after remaining in the same job for many years, you may begin to feel dulled by the same responsibilities.

You may lose the initial enthusiasm and your work may feel tedious and drab. If you remain flexible towards learning, you will be drawn towards upskilling, not only in your core domain but in other areas as well. Learning new skills will help you get exposed to new subjects and areas that might renew your interest in your job. As you proceed into adulthood, you have to understand that the market is always evolving. There would always be new tricks to the trade that you may learn to reignite your passion towards work.

Upskilling has become an integral part of meeting the never-ending demands of life. Learning new skills will make you more efficient at fulfilling your responsibilities by increasing your knowledge and expertise on subjects and tools associated with your work life. You are more likely to improve your job security if you outperform yourself every year.

Technology is forever evolving and there is a constant demand to keep pace with it. If you do not keep up with the changing times, you are at a higher risk of losing many opportunities. Learning something new invariably prepares you for the future. You may not have travelled by train in your whole life, but once you overcome the mental block against it and gain the new experience, you are better prepared for similar challenges in life. Learning new skills helps not only in the growth of your career but also in accelerating your personal development.

By regularly attending courses and workshops that help in increasing your knowledge repository, you will become more aware of the new trends in the market and new developments in your niche area. You become more disciplined in the course of mastering a new skill and this improved discipline has positive impact on other aspects of your life as well. There is a particular trend in India. Everyone wants to grab a management degree and opt for a managerial position. They spend two-three years in their core domain and then slowly shift to an administrative role. Such situations are not very common in the western world.

In the USA, a software developer remains the same and keeps upskilling in the same field with newer technologies. The idea is to become a better version of yourself and remain competitive in the changing world. However, in India, there is an undying urge to abandon your core domain only to become a manager. While you do earn a lot of money as a manager, you tend to overlook the changing scenario in your core domain, and over the years, you may fail to realize what you have lost. Upskilling yourself indeed opens a whole new avenue for you to climb the ladder of success.

With the right skills, you can apply for higher-level jobs that will give you better pay, work environment and responsibilities. However, if you wish to change the domain of your job, you have to go for reskilling to learn skills related to a completely new job discipline, master the basic skills required for that domain and upskill yourself from there. Enhancing your knowledge includes both upskilling and reskilling, and this in turn helps you to realize your dreams sooner than you expect.

Hunger Must Remain Forever

"The important thing is not to stop questioning. Curiosity has its own reason for existing. One cannot help but be in awe when he contemplates the mysteries of eternity, of life, of the marvelous structure of reality. It is enough if one tries merely to comprehend a little of this mystery every day. Never lose a holy curiosity." – Albert Einstein

A curious mind is an architect of invention; a brewer of change. If you look around the world of inventions and discoveries, you will find how curiosity to understand the unknown has led to some marvelous innovations in the world. The world is full of wonders, all you need is a mind that knows how to admire them and marvel at them.

Winston Churchill's life is a wonderful example of how curiosity for learning new things turned an otherwise lazy little wretch into a historical figure of our times. In 1895, when his father passed away, a 21-year-old Winston stood at the crossroads of life. His father often used to accuse him of being a wastrel. He had to choose a path to prove his father wrong. As a soldier, he survived the trauma of battle and escaped capture during the Second Boer War. As a writer, he penned fifteen books, countless essays and newspaper articles, and eventually won the Nobel Prize in Literature.

As a public servant, he served in the Parliament for sixty-four years and was appointed to ten ministerial positions including the post of Chancellor of the Exchequer and Prime Minister on two occasions. As a statesman, he made extraordinarily difficult decisions which saved Great Britain during the Second World War. Churchill's academic eminence was never worth mentioning. Moreover, he never possessed an illustrious degree on political science to get a hold on the political history of the world. However, he could become a statesman of high caliber by learning from the many challenges that he faced throughout his formative years.

Those early trials taught Churchill the importance of diligence, ambition and hard work. These, in turn, helped him discover a love of learning that enabled him to think beyond the mistakes of the past and to the solutions for the future. The more you learn, the more you are enabled to exercise discernment in the matters of choosing between the right and wrong. Whether life gifts you success or throws you in the dungeon of failure, your ability to withstand the change and openness to learn something new shall take you to new heights in life. Once you align your mind with knowledge, you invariably add profits to your pocket in some or the other way.

When I had enrolled for my Executive Programme for General Management (EPGM) from MIT, Boston, I was initially overwhelmed by the course details. A 10 months programme, 36 modules and a truckload of assignments! A doubt did gnaw at me for a couple of days whether I would be able to finish the course or not.

Instead of limiting myself with unwarranted doubts, I took the plunge and started the course. In times to come, I had to travel to Boston, Kuala Lumpur, Singapore and Vietnam. Assignments, talks, presentations, and yet I was mesmerized by the challenges thrown at me. I could readily grab the opportunity of interacting with different people. Cultural differences, language barrier and knowledge gap, everything seemed to have vanished before my eagerness to learn. I could have a practical experience of business challenges coupled with cultural conflict. Once I had dropped my inhibitions, I could walk on the path of ever new experiences. As Neale Donald Walsch, the American author once said, *"Life begins at the end of your comfort zone."*

Trying new things and venturing into new avenues of learning is undoubtedly daunting. The unfamiliar makes us nervous in an indefinable way. Leaving our comfort zone brings us in a vulnerable position, and troubles us with a number of questions running through our heads. We keep on questioning if we should do this or would we make a mockery of ourselves by doing this. Moreover, we let the fear of uncertainty stop us.

But forcing ourselves out of our comfort zones is good for us. Trying new things is not only helpful in conquering those fears, but it also allows us to expand our minds and learn about new things, and about ourselves. In fact, psychological research has proved that people who engage in a variety of experiences are more likely to retain positive emotions and remain motivated than people who have fewer experiences. The moment you decide to gain more knowledge, you try out new skills and open yourself to new emotions, experiences, and cultures. Honestly, isn't it boring to keep recycling the same old things over and over again?

> *"The beginning of knowledge is the discovery of something we do not understand."*
> – Frank Herbert

Adding a new feature to your life's portfolio just makes your life more interesting. One always tends to gain by learning more. Investing in gaining knowledge is quite like investing in a blue-chip company – the growth trajectory is always upwards.

PART B
A FAIL-PROOF PLAN TO SURVIVE

6

CATCHING THE BUS

So, why do some people come late for a lecture or miss a train and regularly piss off their friends and colleagues? Always being late is an art, a frustrating and inconvenient art to say the least. Or shall I call it a personality trait?

We all live in a time-crunched world while jostling with each other to reach the pinnacle of success, and in this struggle to excel in life, unpunctuality becomes a potential red flag. Valuing time is one of the key teachings we all are taught from the very beginning of our academic career. We all know how time plays a crucial role in getting a job or exceling in an examination or even in building relationships. Time is one of the most precious ingredients for our overall growth in life.

Whether at professional front or on personal level, time is the essence for achieving success. We have all come across people who are punctual. They are well planned and have their days sorted out in such a way that every minute is accounted for. Punctuality is not just doing a task in time; it is more about doing a task at the right time. However, is it possible to always be on time? After all, life is uncertain and eternally ready to test us.

As the Chinese proverb goes – An inch of time is an inch of gold but you can't buy that inch of time with an inch of gold. The fickle nature of time is well known to us and still only a handful of people realize the true value of being punctual. Do you have a friend who always comes late to a gathering, and when you ask him, he is always ready with an excuse? It is indeed true that none of us can control what life has planned for us. We may have sorted out everything but what if an emergency crops up all of a sudden. Let's say you are all set for your job interview which is scheduled at 10. You have planned well in time and have decided to catch the local train at 8. You are sure of reaching the venue by 9.30. Great!

You get on the train, but as it crosses three stations, it stops in the middle of nowhere due to a technical fault. You look at your watch and realize that you still have enough time to reach the venue, for the train will not be left abandoned like this in the middle of nowhere for long. Half an hour passes by and you don't find the train moving. What should you do now? You can no longer make it on time. So, is that all? Will you miss this job opportunity? The answer would have been yes if you were living in the 90's, which is not the case. You can always pick up your mobile phone and inform the organizer about this difficulty that you have come across. Believe me, if your resume is good enough, you will be given that chance to join at a later time.

Running into unexpected situations is a part and parcel of life. We never know when an unfortunate incident would befall us and put us in a fix. In that aforementioned case scenario, you could have simply waited for the train to move without informing your interviewer. What would have happened? You would have reached late and cited the problem after reaching the venue.

However, that would have created a distinct image of your personality trait. The interviewer would have already put a cross in front of your time management and interpersonal skills. If we look at the broader picture, time management and interpersonal skills are vital factors for every employee.

You may be the greatest coder of your time, but what is the use if you cannot produce the desired outcome well within time? There is no big deal in missing the bus once in a while, but when you put that extra effort of letting the other person know about your delay, you add value to the relationship.

> *"Time is what we want most, but what we use worst."*
> – William Penn

You're Excused, But Not Always

Unpunctuality has a kind of Domino Effect. When you are late for one thing, it makes you late for every next thing that is in your to-do list. Once in a while, things may go out of your hands and you may end up being late. The sudden change in your plans shall be taken into consideration by your friends, family or peers once or twice. However, when you make it a habit of being late all the time, no one is going to lend their ears to your excuses. You will be tagged as an unpunctual person who undervalues the time of others.

Let me share a little fact about my habits. I would like to talk about my way of managing time. I place my trust in getting practical experiences rather than learning things from a book. My entrepreneurial journey was on a patchy street filled with potholes. Without first getting into the field, there was no way of erecting a business model like iKure. So, to be on the ground, I had to consider many aspects all at once. I had to attend conferences, shuffle through the details of prospective clients, meet people from different strata of life, and then there always remained a long list of speaker invitations and panel discussions to be taken care of. Now, every aforementioned segment is crucial for my growth and the growth of my company. I am not given a choice to prioritize one and abandon the others. Moreover, when I am given so much importance to be a part of a panel discussion or to be a speaker for an event, I cannot afford to be late. If I reach late, the event would start late, thereby jeopardizing everyone's schedule.

So, is it like when you become someone great, then only you should value time? The answer is a resounding NO. To become someone great, you have to learn the essence and beauty of time management. Mr. Ratan Tata is never late for any meeting. Whether it is about meeting his board members or sitting for an interview, he is always on time. You may argue that established people like Tata and Birla have so many assistants to get their job done and that is why they can always be on time. However, it is not entirely true. Being a leader, when they stick to their time schedule, they set an example for their subordinates. Once the chief is on time, no subordinate can ever be late. A leader's ability to manage time effectively induces everyone in the team to follow the same route.

Unpunctuality is a bad habit that can hit your growth the hardest. When you lose value of time, you invariably reduce your efficiency. Let's see a hypothetical scenario. You are pursuing your college degree and have been given an assignment to finish. You check on the deadline and feel relieved on seeing that you have two weeks' time on hand. Though the assignment is simple and you could finish it in a couple of days, you put it on the backburner presuming you have ample time in hand.

You waste a week doing nothing concrete and eventually forget about the assignment. As one of your friends asks about the status of your assignment, you are reminded about it and decide to finish it within the next two days. However, you face a family emergency all of a sudden and fail to submit the assignment on time. It is your first time and the professor gives you another chance. But you don't learn anything from the situation and remain lackadaisical in your approach. Giving excuses becomes your habit and it doesn't go unnoticed by your professors. Eventually you end up getting bad remarks and also fail to score good marks.

Let's see the same situation from a different perspective. You have always been an average student and somehow got into the company of brilliant minds while pursuing your college degree. Once you see your friends excelling in examinations through effective time management, you too adopt this habit and start planning things out.

Over a period of time, your scores improve and you become more efficient. So, how could you come out of that lackadaisical approach? Your friends are not some great achievers or renowned figures in the society. They are commoners just like you. However, they could set an example for you to follow which made you unlock your true potential.

If you take my example of pursuing that management degree from MIT, I was initially burdened by the number of assignments, classes and travelling to different countries. But, once I took the plunge, I couldn't come out. I had to plan everything in such a way that it didn't affect my routine work. I too had only 24 hours to manage everything, and I could have easily termed my situation as impossible. But then, I took a different lens to observe the situation. The benefits of that MIT degree weighed more than the struggle to manage time. Once you stop ambling in the aisle of excuses, you find the hidden opportunities in every task you take up, and once you discover the opportunities, you surely start making time for everything.

Excusing yourself from a job or meeting someone makes you lose an opportunity to learn something new. When you are young, your life is literally 'happening' and you do not mind missing out an opportunity to meet someone. In your way, it is cool to lead life on your own terms. You can wake up at 10, forget about your appointment with the lecturer or a colleague and presume that no one is looking at these faults or shortcomings. Initially, they do not, but sooner or later your mismanagement of time is noticed and a negative impression is created. Your perspective towards life and your commitment to work come under scrutiny.

Recently, I had the opportunity to go through Bharat Soka Gakkai applications as a judge. It was a commitment out of my regular work routine and I had to invest several hours for shuffling through the applications. I could have easily excused myself from the added responsibility for I already had enough on my plate. However, I look at everything as a source of learning.

As an entrepreneur, I cannot lose on a prospective client and what if attending a particular event gives me that chance. If you do not believe in punctuality, I am sure you must have missed out on meeting somebody significant on many occasions, and as we all know, a chance missed is an opportunity lost.

Are You Managing Your Time Well?

> *"Productivity is never an accident. It is always the result of a commitment to excellence, intelligent planning and focused effort."*
> – Paul J. Meyer

The world watches the efficiency and effectiveness of a successful person; people talk about the success stories; however, they often forget to notice the commitment and strategic planning required to reap the benefits of success. Whether you are attending college or are buried under numerous projects, commitment and focused efforts are your true companions if you wish to excel in life. Once you are sure of your commitment, you tend to plan your schedule wisely and start putting efforts towards achieving the goal. When your efforts are consistent and timely, no one can stop you from achieving success.

I am a man with packed schedules, but none of my team members has ever found the scope to complain about my unavailability. Why? Because I could plan in advance. Am I immune to uncertain moments? No. I do have to make alterations in my plan, but as people have known my efficient time management skills, they never mistake me for a shirker.

Once you prove your punctuality, you are considered as dependable, and believe me, at the start of your career, dependability is a crucial point in your resume. Being on time for work underlines your professionalism. You become a trustworthy and reliable employee when you arrive on time. Moreover, when you are consistently punctual, you raise your bar of efficiency and set an example for the others.

LOSING BIG WINNING BIGGER

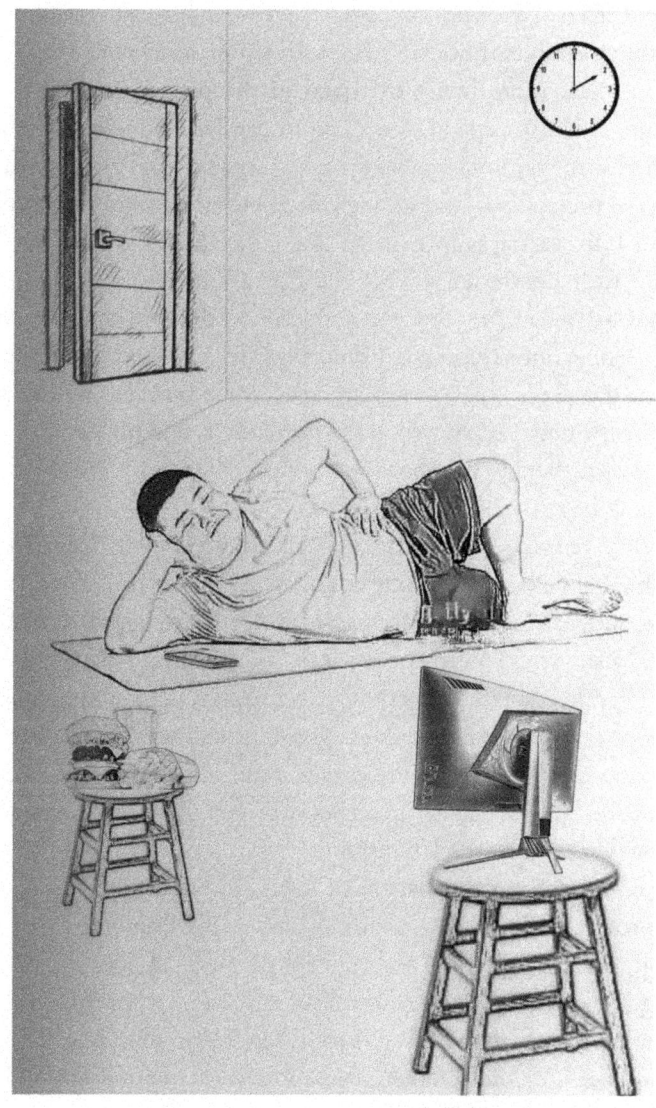

We all are haunted by meeting deadlines. Whether it is for a college assignment or a project for a client, we do strive to meet the deadlines to preserve our prestige. Punctuality and effective time management ensure meeting deadlines on time.

Let us assume you are a content creator and have three projects in hand. Two of your projects are relatively easy and you could finish it within a couple of hours. You look at your watch and heave, for you have six more hours to spend in the office. You have two options; either you spend (waste) time near that coffee machine and chitchat with your other colleagues or you can sit and brainstorm on the third project. So, am I asking you to become a workaholic? No.

All I am asking is to manage time efficiently to avoid that last minute rush. Let me tell you how I efficiently manage my early hours of the day. When I hit the gym and walk on the treadmill, my mind keeps typing out all the essential emails I have to send for the day. I dissect out every email inside my head while burning my calories. And by the time I reach my desk, I need not sit and brainstorm over what to write and how to be effective through my words. I am in the saddle to do the job.

While running the rat race, we all are competing against time which invariably leaves us stressed. If you fail to manage your time well and remain late for your assignments, you are bound to feel the rush. By showing up early or on time, you can give yourself enough time to complete tasks at a comfortable pace. Moreover, punctuality helps you improve your work relationships and teamwork. Arriving to work on time proves that you respect others' time, which undeniably improves their perception of you. And this holds good even in your personal relationships.

An effective time management helps you balance your personal and professional life. You can be as busy as the Prime Minister, but if you cannot make time for your loved ones, all your efforts are going in vain. Irrespective of my busy schedule, I never miss talking to my mother every morning. Yes. Every single morning, I talk to my mother. For the younger generation, it may sound funny for a middle-aged man to talk to his mother every day.

However, if you consider time as the most precious element of life, you have to keep aside the time you must have with your loved ones. Once they are gone, you can never go back in time and talk to them or meet them.

Relationships are built and destroyed based on the time you invest in them. You are young and of course looking at a progressive career, but you can never deny the significance of personal and professional relationships. You have to be present when someone close to you needs your time and attention. Being punctual helps you follow your own schedule by allowing you to complete all your work during work hours. By arriving to work late, you risk missing meetings and getting behind on important tasks, which may mean working outside of normal hours. Being on time can help you work on or ahead of schedule and reserve your free time for other things and it ensures you go home on time, which helps you keep a healthy work-life balance. You have a win-win situation where both professional and personal lives remain on track.

When you manage your time properly and successfully meet your deadlines, you tend to feel a sense of fulfillment which adds greatly to your confidence. Consistently finishing your daily to-do list is a huge motivator that drives you to further improve your time management skills and take on new work opportunities. Moreover, when you are happy and content in your work life, you will not take work inside your personal domain and your personal life remains unaffected by the work pressure.

The core idea of managing time effectively is to improve our overall productivity and social involvement. Once we manage time well, we open a door to learning something new. We get time to ponder upon our existing knowledge and try out new modes to build on it. As Peter Drucker rightly said – Knowledge has to be improved, challenged, and increased constantly, or it vanishes.

The Art Of Multitasking

No human is built or can ever work for 24 hours round the clock. However, an effective management of time can help in completing both personal and professional commitments. Managing your time well imparts you with the ability to balance multiple tasks and in turn, improve your life and career.

You must know your priorities well. I can chair a multinational conglomerate, but I cannot ignore a team member who has some crucial things to discuss. Amid my hectic schedule, I do make time for my team who need my opinion or involvement. Multitasking is useful in enhancing your productivity, which in turn will help in reaching important goals and advancing your career.

Are you able to manage multiple responsibilities at once by focusing on one task while keeping track of others? If yes, you are doing a great job. Multitasking is not about losing focus on the job at hand and getting distracted by other queued up assignments. In your workplace, you will often find some of your colleagues switching back and forth between tasks and effectively performing different tasks rapidly one after the other.

I am not saying you should multitask like launching a rocket and sending business emails all at once. Have you seen receptionists at hospitals and diagnostic centers? They are able to answer the phone calls while diligently managing other tasks at hand. Multitasking is an art which comes with a number of benefits. Let us assume you are having a call with a client. Can you not take down some notes while speaking to the client? You can, and while you take down the notes, your brain plays the wonder game of joining the dots and you could add some more questions to the discussion and make it more productive.

So, in the same span of time, you could complete two tasks simultaneously. Interestingly, as an entrepreneur myself, I do look for people who can multitask. You can delegate more tasks to a multitasker without worrying about the quality of the output. Multitasking helps you feel more effective because when you complete more tasks than expected from you, there prevails a sense of fulfillment. It becomes a source of motivation for you and you work harder to achieve your goals.

How can you learn the art of multitasking? I have always been a multitasker, but it does take time to hone this skill. You have to learn the skill of organization. You must know exactly what tasks you need to complete and when to complete them.

Organizing includes managing your day, week and month to keep you on track with your tasks. I have often seen people with a messy worktable. I am not finicky about cleanliness but I want you to know the benefits of proper organization.

Let us talk about a hypothetical case scenario. Rohit is a young recruit and is superb at his job. None of his colleagues can perform at coding better than him. However, he is a little messy. He tends to forget where he keeps official papers. He may be a great coder but can never follow the deadlines as he is never organized. While Anil, another fresh recruit, is very meticulous. Not only his files and worktable look tidy, but also his computer screen. Every client file is tagged and meticulously organized. He can always finish a given task before the deadline because he never has to shuffle through hundreds of papers or files to know the requirements. Not even a single day has he overworked, while Rohit spends half the days shuffling through the clients' demands. Within a year, Anil is given a promotion for his ability to manage everything well in time. By virtue of being organized in his life, he could also devote reasonable time to his family.

You must be relating organization with Sheldon Cooper from the Big Bang Theory. No, I am not asking anyone to go to that extreme. All I say is organize well enough to know your priorities. You should master the skill to assess your responsibilities and organize tasks in terms of importance to manage your time. In a day, you may have ten tasks to finish and you could be in a dilemma which one to do first. People could handle such a situation in two different ways. Some may prioritize the difficult tasks over the simpler ones, while some may go the other way round.

Let us assume, you have two assignments to finish within a day. One seems easy as the subject is known to you, while the other belongs to a course which is not your forte. As the latter is going to be time consuming, you may choose to do it later. Regardless of how you choose to prioritize, the ability to maximize your output by creating order is a necessary skill for effective multitasking. Are you in the habit of scheduling things in advance?

If no, inculcate that. A habit of planning ahead is beneficial right from the beginning of your career. Switching from a lucrative career to a hectic life of an entrepreneur was not easy. I had to plan everything in advance, whether meeting clients or hiring the right team. The process of scheduling helped me analyze complex situations and break them down into manageable steps and deadlines. If you are able to plan your day-to-day activities, and account for unexpected tasks, you can always multitask to stay on schedule. Making a to-do list often helps in segregating what is urgent and what is not. After you organize and prioritize your tasks, group together similar tasks.

Multitasking usually involves working on similar duties, so grouping them together can increase your efficiency. It is something like combining tasks that require the same actions, such as working on social media campaigns for three different accounts. By working on related tasks, you can increase your concentration.

The art of multitasking is not about increasing the number of working hours in a day but improving the effectiveness of each passing moment, and this can be achieved well if you reduce your distractions. Instead of swiping through random forwarded messages in WhatsApp, you can have a few breaks to recharge your energy. The idea is to be productive without losing on time. Have you ever faced a situation of a delayed flight?

Bad weather or technical faults often cause delays in flights and if one flight is delayed, it has a Domino effect on the other flights too. Every event in life is interconnected with each other. Any disruption in one of the events cause trouble in the whole sequence. When you are capable of multitasking, you are abled enough to keep a track of every event and can keep everything within the timeframe and thus you can avoid any delay.

Time: The Most Expensive Gift

Ratan Tata is one the most phenomenal figures in our country. He has built the Tata Empire and holds a long list of loyal employees.

Whether he was overtaking Ford's Land Rover market or was a guest of honor in a conference, no one could ever complain about compromised timeliness. It is because he believes in the value of time. Sticking to the schedule not only helps in preserving your time but also helps you value others' time.

When I started off as an entrepreneur, Jayesh Parekh, co-founder of Sony Entertainment Television, was one of my first angel investors. To be honest, the entrepreneurial journey is hectic, and most of the times, you end up working 24 by 7. I often had to meet him for business purposes and he used to give me a time slot of 9 AM. Believe me, not a single day was I ever late for the meeting. I used to be present by 8:55 AM. Here, I am not boasting about my punctuality, I'm trying to emphasize about valuing others' time.

As a youngster, you may feel like laughing away the idea of punctuality and very often trying to run it down with a statement like Let me enjoy life. True, one must enjoy life to the fullest. However, enjoying one's life can never be synonymous to wasting time. Scrolling down through Facebook feeds, watching brainless reels on Instagram, do you find any purpose in those? Instead of wasting time on sites like those, you can always try to learn something new, cultivate a hobby or just engage in some family time. If you wish to have a successful life with a sense of fulfillment, you have to invest your time in constructive activities. Never confuse a constructive activity with a tedious job. Instead of scrolling down your mobile screen, how about spending some quality time with your aged grandparents?

We all learned one proverb in school – Time and tide wait for none. It highlights the importance of making the right decision at the right time. Once you delay making a decision, the opportunity may pass you by. Time is free for all, but can you buy or sell time? A river flows ahead, it does not come back. You can grow older but cannot become any younger. You can recover lost wealth but time once lost can never be regained. During my early days of building iKure, I had to visit Delhi quite often. Once I had a packed schedule with three or four meetings within a short span of time.

I had finished a meeting by 1 in the afternoon and then checked on my schedule. Another meeting was at 2. I had a quick lunch and started looking for a conveyance to reach the meeting spot. In those days, Uber and Ola were not so popular and I had to rely on a rickshaw fellow. Even then, at that weird time of the day when everyone wishes to have a quick nap, it was not easy for me to convince that rickshaw puller. I had my luggage and laptop bag to carry and I couldn't afford to miss the scheduled meeting. Convincing him was nothing less than a herculean task. However, I was determined. Even along with my luggage and laptop bag, I did not fear to travel in a rickshaw for I could not afford to miss that meeting. It all essentially boils down to your determination. I could have left that opportunity considering the kind of inflexible negotiation I was doing with the rickshaw puller. However, I was firm to convince him at any cost because my ultimate goal was to conclude the meeting.

Sticking to the schedule requires a lot of commitment. You can find students or employees dishing out multiple excuses when faced with such a situation. It is a common habit amongst people to leave a task for the next day. Let me ask you if you know what is stored for you tomorrow? Many a times, employees promise their clients some unrealistic deadlines. This too is a common practice and especially in the world of entrepreneurship.

While chasing the title of 'The best man in the market', many entrepreneurs set unrealistic goals without giving two hoots to the volatile nature of life. Setting a time frame for others is like kindling hope in them to receive the desired outcome within that time. Let us say, you have promised your housemaid an increment by the next month. She keeps making plans about buying something essential which she could not till date. But then, you forget about your proposal of increasing her salary and as a result, all her plans are shattered. Time is precious because life is short. We never know what will happen in the next moment. We know how much money is there in our bank balance, but we do not know how much time is left with us.

Time waits for no one. When you are struck by failure, you realize the value of time. Do you want to know the value of one year? Just ask a student who failed a course. If you want to know the value of one month, talk to a mother who delivered her baby prematurely. The importance of a minute can be learned from a person who missed the flight by one minute and had to postpone his whole journey.

Do you want to know the value of one second? Ask the person who just escaped death in a car accident. In case you doubt about the value of one-hundredth of a second, think about the athlete who lost the Olympic Gold by that miniscule margin.

"Your time is limited, so don't waste it living someone else's life. Don't be trapped by dogma - which is living with the results of other people's thinking. Don't let the noise of other's opinions drown out your own inner voice. And most important, have the courage to follow your heart and intuition. They somehow already know what you truly want to become. Everything else is secondary."

– Steve Jobs

On 12th of June, 2005, Steve Jobs addressed the convocation for a graduating batch. He delivered a mesmerizing talk through three stories. The story that particularly touched everyone was his third story about death. He had already been diagnosed with Cancer. His words echoed in the gathering when he uttered that all external expectations, pride, fear of embarrassment or failure would just fall away in the face of death. One would just leave behind a legacy. He said, *"Remembering that you are going to die is the best way I know to avoid the trap of thinking you have something to lose. You are already naked. There is no reason not to follow your heart."*

Once he had been diagnosed with the terminal illness, the doctors simply asked him to be prepared for death. Jobs did prepare for a life which was uncertain. He underwent a surgery for his rare form of pancreatic cancer in order to be relieved of pain.

However, if you go through the details about his life after the diagnosis, you can see that he did not dwell on the inevitable. He kept moving with time and did what he could with the time he was left with.

The wheel of time is never going to stop for anyone. With a life so uncertain, you will get hundreds of opportunities and will also fall flat with failures. With so many distractions hovering around, managing time in a productive way may often seem like an endless struggle.

With each phase of success and failure, you will realize the true value of time. Your future depends on what you do today and not on what you reserve for tomorrow. It is always easy to build a solid chain of excuses, but have you ever pondered upon what you lose by mismanaging time? You are all given a blank canvas of life to paint it with good memories, success stories and new learnings. Keep up with this fast-paced life where every second matters. Who knows that missing a bus could lose you a bright career?

"Time Management is a misnomer; the challenge is to manage ourselves."
— Stephen Covey

7

AWAKEN THE DON WITHIN YOU

"I learned that courage was not the absence of fear, but the triumph over it. The brave man is not he who does not feel afraid, but he who conquers that fear."
– Nelson Mandela

Life is more like a righteous cycle of humble beginnings and magnificent ends. In the proverbial way, the good gets good and the evil faces the consequences. However, life is not demarcated between black and white, it is multihued with a plethora of emotions. No matter how good you have been, you are bound to face evil and believe me, every bad incident is going to add to the overall experience in your life. We all share the objective to grow better with each passing day and in this pursuit, we keep trying out different things.

In short, if you desire for something; you have to kick-start the process. You may fail in your attempts or may end up achieving a glorious success worth showcasing. However, when you begin something new in life, you are bound to be deterred by the miasma of uncertainties. You fear because you are neither aware of the outcome nor you know the consequences of your efforts. There are a number of factors at work - environmental conditions, society at large and its fickle reaction and what not.

The uncertainty is always there — it is a given and even though we all know that life is uncertain, we are engulfed by an unperishable fear. We are scared of failing. We fear loss, rejection and loneliness. We are scared of looking foolish. As the best-selling author Stephen King has said, "The scariest moment is always just before you start. After that, things can only get better." There is no bigger fear than the fear of failing in our endeavors and that of unknown challenges. While we bargain with uncertainties in life, we often forget that once we dare facing those challenges, we develop an altered perspective towards success and failure.

Scripting success needs the special ink of courage. Life will remain uncertain, come what may. However, once you inhale courage and brace yourself to face the adverse situations, you already accomplish writing half of your success story. We often see people succeeding in life - an auto driver's daughter clearing the CA examination, a young middle-class man succeeding in his entrepreneurial pursuit or a physically challenged person climbing a peak and breaking records.

When we read through these success stories, we often conclude that all these successful people belong to a clan to whom success probably comes in handy. Or we just assume that they are the lucky ones getting a competitive edge by fluke. Ha! Is it possible? There is no scenario in which success is brewed easily. When I say it is okay to fail, I also emphasize on the need for courage to get up and pursue your dream all over again. We are all equipped to achieve something extraordinary in life - to get the big wins, to exceed expectations and deliver to our highest standards.

As life moves on and puts us through the never-ending string of challenges, we are often asked to upgrade our goals. It is never an easy task to change your goals halfway, but with a dose of courage, you develop confidence to see through the challenges in an altered way. What if you wish to surf one of those gigantic waves, stand on the board through that blue, swirling tunnel?

There lies a mile between what you wish for and what you do in life. I can sit at home, watch those cottony clouds floating on the sky, hum a mellifluous song and dream of becoming the next Sonu Nigam or Arijit Singh. However, is it possible to become something worth talking by simply sitting at home? Never. If you wish to get something in life, you have to start putting efforts towards achieving your goal. Believe me, no one on this planet knows the outcome of their efforts. Not even Einstein could know the probability of success as he pursued framing the theory of relativity. Your wish to do anything in life must be followed by intrepid efforts. The more you fear about the final outcome, the more you are pulled away from your goal.

However, fear is inevitable for it is ingrained in our biological makeup. No one can be utterly fearless in life as fear has been a natural response mechanism of humankind. However, courage remains the secret potion that allows you to act despite your fears. Courage gives you the ability to put aside your fear of failure and take the first step. It allows you to attempt things that you have not tried before despite your fear of looking foolish.

Let us assume that you have an interview today with a huge multinational conglomerate. You do possess all the necessary qualifications and skills, but you are scared because of the huge status of the company. A chain of doubts keeps pulling you down and you hesitate to attend the interview itself. You doubt your abilities as the company's reputation clouds your thinking. Now, let me ask you a simple question. If you were not worthy enough, why did the company choose to interview you? Instead of doubting your abilities, if you decide to embrace courage, you would be able to see the situation through a cleaner lens.

If you dig deeper into this situation, you would realize that your initial fear has subsided. In reality, you do not fear the big conglomerate but are scared of the people within it. No?

People: The Real Cause of Our Fear

There is a famous quote by the famous mathematician Alfred North Whitehead – True courage is not the brutal force of vulgar heroes, but the firm resolve of virtue and reason. Whenever we think of gathering courage to move ahead in life, our inherent fearful nature warns us about people's reaction on our failure. Is it not? Of course, everything revolves around what others would say about us. Let us say you are bored of your corporate job and desire to be your own boss. You wish to become an entrepreneur and spend a couple of years chalking out every detail of the process. One fine day, as you declare your plans of leaving the lucrative corporate job and begin something of your own, all hell breaks loose at home. Your father fails to fathom your logic behind leaving the stable job and your mother starts worrying about your future married life. Does it sound familiar? It may not be the case with rich families but definitely strikes a chord in the heart of a working-class family. We mainly fear to hurt the prescribed norms of the society. We fear the people around us. What will they say about us if we take an unconventional path? It is this fear that shatters our confidence to deal with different situations of life.

When we talk about challenges in life, let me warn you that many challenges are made of flesh and blood. Facing a bully is one of the biggest challenges in life as it scars our emotional wellbeing which is crucial for our growth. As a child, we are often taught to ignore the bullies as our parents consider them a harmless part of growing up. The same continues in college life and in professional life too. We often get so used to bullying that we declare ourselves weaker against those dominating characters in our life. Usually, a child is bullied physically or verbally, but with advancement in age, bullying becomes more indirect.

No matter which lane of life we choose to walk in, bullies are inevitable. Trust me, you are not alone in this torturous game. There are many famous personalities who faced bullying. Muhammad Ali was a young kid when a bully took away his bike. When he reported it to a cop, the latter asked him to learn boxing in order to get his bike back. As we all know, the rest is history!

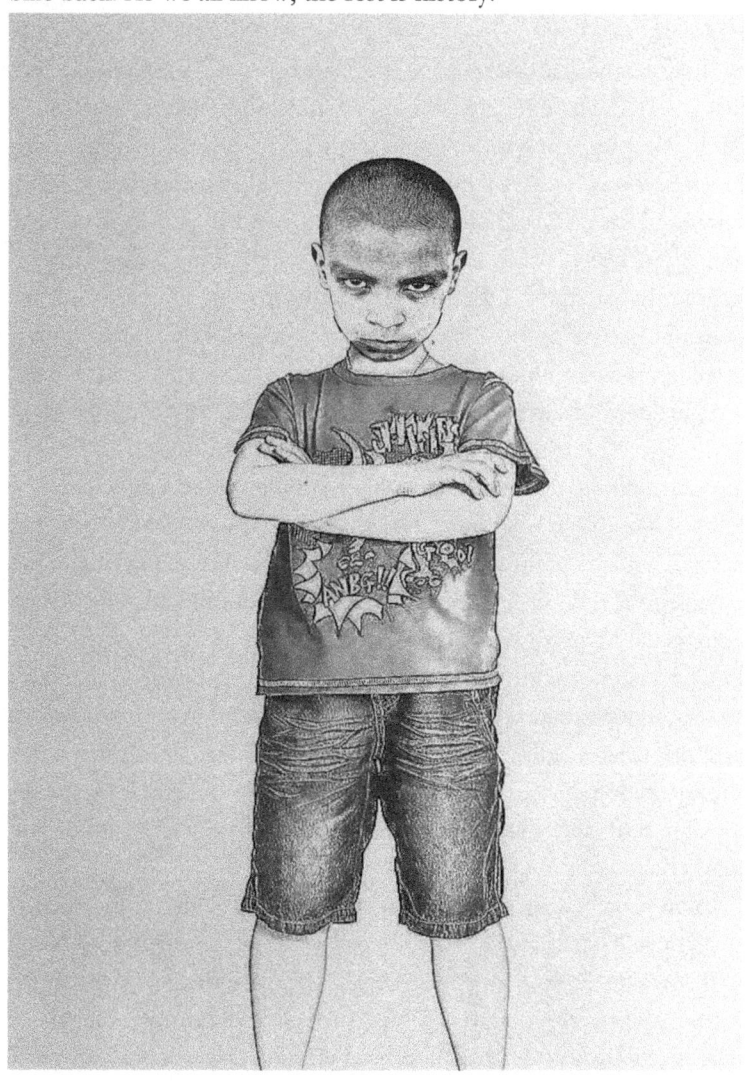

Now, bullying is inevitable and omnipresent. Whether you live in a small village of Africa or in Washington DC, you will be deprived of your sanity by people's unsolicited remarks. It is unavoidable for you cannot control anyone's opinion about you. You can however, brace yourself against such challenges. We all come into this world as weaklings but have the potential to build a reservoir of courage in our lives.

Let me share a crucial incident from my life. Those days, I was just another corporate job holder who was doing everything possible to reach the company's ultimate goal. A higher official, who happened to be one of the board members, did not maintain the minimum decorum of a healthy workplace. I was new in my career and often lost control of my emotions as I did not know how to handle the situation. I knew I was doing my job as instructed but constant questioning and harassment by a senior member started affecting my confidence and productivity.

This kind of situation is not uncommon. We are taught to fear authority. We are injected with the habit of not raising our voice against anything that has been done by a senior. Get a survey on any kind of workplace and you will be amazed by the number of bullying cases. While confidence is the dividend of encountering the unexpected and dealing successfully with it over and over again, courage is the premium you pay to reap the benefits of confidence. Let us assume that you have been performing really well in the technical department of your office and considering your hard work and persuasion skills, the management decides to promote you to the marketing department. You are happy for you are going to get an appraisal and many other fringe benefits once you join the marketing team.

You have been good in your technical domain and thus presume that you will perform the same way in the new department too. Now, is this a sign of courage? No. This is overconfidence. You cannot relate apples with oranges. Courage is exhibited when you decide to take up the role after upskilling yourself with all the skills that fit in the marketing department.

Courage is when you decide to be calm and poised with the new assignment and do not fear to learn new things in life. One of the major problems that rules our mindset is that we often think of handling situations but hardly think of handling people around us who are the ones instigating fear in us. Whether you are in college or you are freshly appointed in a company, you enter the premises with bookish knowledge. You know how to finish an assignment; you are aware of your role and job description and given a chance you can finish your duties with flying colors. But, let me ask you if you are prepared for the people you are going to face? Half of the adverse situations are triggered by people's behavior towards you.

Let us say you are in the middle of a project and working out a critical part and suddenly you are being called in for another work by your boss. The next work that has been bestowed upon you is quite difficult for you to accomplish, but you fear to reveal that to your boss as he seems to be miffed by something. You take up the load and promise to finish the task within the given timeframe. You slog day and night for completing two different projects within the same timeframe. In a couple of days, you have a nervous breakdown for the tasks were beyond your reach. Once you fail to achieve, your boss humiliates you in front of everyone which shakes up your confidence.

Now, over a period of time, you keep losing your efficiency because you start living in constant fear. What if you fail again? What if the boss humiliates you again? You are haunted by an unnerving feeling that all your colleagues have watched you getting scolded. So, what is new in all this waffling? I am just leasing out the facts of workplace culture which every young aspirant should know. But is knowing going to solve the problem? You may know about your toxic boss but knowing his offensive attitude will not protect you from his wrath. Will it?

You have to strategize to face him. You have to chalk out an effective plan to deal with toxic work culture. Moreover, as you cross different stages of life, you fathom the presence of masked human nature. An otherwise friendly colleagues will be backstabbing you. While a not so talkative peer is actually doing something good for you. Initially, you will be unable to see the true colors of a person but as you comprehend the disguised politics of parasitic competition, you will have to strategize your actions.

In my long career, I have witnessed young and dynamic minds leaving their job due to bad working conditions and lethal corporate culture. Some left because they got better opportunities, and they did not wish to lose their sanity over wrong people, while some others left because of fear of humiliation which is not a good sign for career development. You have to understand that leaving something bad never eliminates the fear of getting embraced by the bad again. The point is, how far can you run away? Can you leave every job by the slightest of the pricky moments? You cannot afford to. The only way out is to face your fear with a poised temperament.

Let us revisit the previous case scenario. You are in the middle of a critical assignment and your boss burdens you with another task. Instead of keeping mum, you strike a fruitful conversation and let your boss know about the impossible demand. What will happen? Assume the worst scenario. You will be bombarded and will be asked to work overtime. Instead of falling apart, you decide to give a try by working to your maximum potential without breaking down. You manage to finish the first task as you had set that as your priority. The second task is not finished and you go back to your boss and request for an extended timeline. He might frown for a moment, but once he sees that you could divide your time well to reach a manageable state for both the tasks, he will realize your credibility.

The crucial point is to remain truthful towards your endeavor. We cannot deny that shirkers are prevalent in every workplace who mostly come to office to have free WI-FI and coffee. And bosses invariably end up thinking that every other employee is an escapist. However, if you are truthful towards your work and well aware of your potential, you need not be afraid of what others think about you.

If you have been consistent in your efforts and are well-versed with the kind of tasks you can accomplish within a specific timeframe, you can always be open about it. Initially, people may presume that you are avoiding and you will be criticized for that. You cannot take the criticism as humiliation. You should strive harder with a calm head and prove yourself right. When you are young, it indeed sounds risky to point out the wrongdoings of an authoritative figure. Whether it is about correcting an esteemed professor or parents or boss, the process of correcting others is unnerving because not everyone is magnanimous enough to accept their mistakes. Still, if you express your point with confidence, you can indeed bring in the necessary changes.

It all depends on how you present yourself. A calm and composed individual has a better grip over any situation than an impulsive and emotionally intolerant person. Love and Kindness are never wasted. They always make a difference. They bless the one who receives them and they bless you, the giver, said the famous American author, Barbara De Angelis.

However, this fast-paced life has become analogous to how people try to escape drowning. They always push the other person down to get outside the water. No? Love and kindness are the assets of human nature, but they do not serve the purpose when troublemakers are overpowering you relentlessly. If people ignore your mellifluous flute, you have to beat the drum to make yourself audible enough. Sooner or later, people around you will realize the value of your words.

As you mature in life, you gradually realize that the courage you possess defines you. Courage lets us expand our life, abilities, and responsibilities. Our potential is directly proportional to our courage. How? To accomplish practically anything in life, you have to awaken the don within you. If you have no courage, you will shrink from trying something new, and you will have great difficulty picking yourself up to try again after failing. In my case, I would say that it was a gradual process of learning the strategies to tackle difficult people. The board member did try to take me for granted.

It was I who had to draw the line. Gradually, I learned how to extract the positive meaning and abandon the unnecessary comments. That man was great at his work but was unaware of the difficulties faced at the ground level. His expectations were inhuman and insane, and over a period of time, he was made aware of it through my high performance at work. I took charge of my life and career. I set my priorities and believed in my abilities, and gradually everyone could witness what I was capable of.

Limit Your Tolerance Level

> *"Tolerance always has limits, and it cannot tolerate what is itself actively intolerant."*
> – Sidney Hook

There is an undeniable philosophy of life – What we allow, is what will continue. If you let someone dominate you all the times, you are invariably declared submissive and indecisive in life even though you are not. The world sees you the way you show yourself to the world. If you showcase your confidence well, people perceive you as a go-getter, but if you remain in the cocoon of shyness, the world declares you good for nothing.

Consider the same toxic boss - employee scenario. If you let your boss keep on burdening you with inhuman demands without raising a voice, you are simply getting bullied, which is not good for your mental and physical health. There is always a limit to your tolerance. Once or twice, you can face humiliation if you know you have been wrong, but you cannot let every other person take you for granted. Truth to be told, there is a misconstruction in our upbringing.

We are often told to be kind and humble and considerate towards the other person's problems whenever they misbehave. However, there comes a time when we have to put a barrier against ill-mannerism. There will be situations where you are regularly intimidated by a particular coworker without any specific reason.

Just take a break and check if you are repeatedly yelled at, insulted, and put down. Does a coworker talk over you at meetings, criticize you, or steal credit for your work? If this is happening with you, you must abandon the stance of kindness and gratitude and hire the cloak of intolerance. Patience and tolerance are two great assets for growth, but one should know where to limit them.

There will be situations in life where people will badger you unnecessarily with their expert opinions about your personal as well as professional life. Can you shut their mouth? No. But you can indeed become a selective listener. Let us assume a case scenario where you are a freelance content creator. You are bound to get different kinds of clients where some will be well-mannered, understanding and considerate towards the essentialities of your creative job, while some others will knock at your door with insane demands. While you are working, you cannot hasten a process just because the client wants you to. You may end up getting umpteen number of messages from such clients. Is it easy to handle so much unwarranted pressure? No. You will turn mad if you get trapped in that vicious cycle of questioning and responding. A trick that often works wonders during these stressful times is to break the cycle of communication.

Keep a calm head and strategize your responses. Not every action needs immediate reaction. Let's say someone is bombarding you with messages on your WhatsApp. There are two options with you. One is that you check those messages and immediately respond to each and every word scribbled there. While the other option is to not check the messages as you are occupied with something more important. Does it mean that I am asking you to ignore one client and prioritize the other? No. I am asking you to prioritize your response time. Learn to differentiate between your personal and professional time. You cannot let anyone plague your life and other commitments at their whims and fancies. Once you stop yourself from responding immediately, you break the other person's dominance and intrusion in your life.

You do respond but not at their convenience, for you know what is more important to you at that point in time. As you keep breaking the chain of communication, the other person realizes that it is no use trying to extract responses from you every now and then. As you start your career, you will often encounter people who would pick on you and constantly bring your mistakes to attention. Or even worse, you will find someone so full of themselves that they keep gossiping about you, undermining and sabotaging your work. It becomes a herculean task to deal with a bully at work whether you are at the beginning or end of your career. You can advance on the professional growth curve only if you learn how to handle a bully. You have to understand that no bully goes away on their own. Once you make yourself a soft target, you will only encourage the bully. If you tolerate the bully's behavior, you are training the bully to continue with the reprehensible actions.

You may not be able to change how people behave towards you but you can certainly change the way you react to them. If someone is bullying you, you need not reciprocate the same way. You can handle the situation in an affirmative way. You have to welcome constructive criticism to grow in life. You must know which challenge to accept and which to abandon. A few years ago, there was a huge hue and cry over the contents of a book by Shiv Khera. The celebrated author was accused of plagiarism for his book *Freedom is Not Free.*

A retired civil servant, Amrit Lal, dragged Khera to court. The proceedings went on and, in the meantime, Shiv Khera continued with his writings. He defended his writings with his vast research. Despite the court case and out-of-court settlement, Shiv Khera bounced back and continues to remain one of the top writers of motivational books.

As Jeanette Jenkins said – *Never accept other people's limited perception about you. Define yourself. You can do anything.* I remember I was in school when I had to go to Madurai to appear for an examination. My father made me board the train with the necessary things. With no mobile phones at that time, I was completely on my own.

Should I call it harassment? No. Is it because it was my own father who threw that challenge at me? No. I do not consider that incident as a negative one as it helped me grow as a person and learn about my own hidden potential. As the train scurried from

Kharagpur to Madurai, I realized that my father's assessment was correct. I was capable of travelling alone and performed quite well in that examination. Today, as I travel from one country to the other and encounter people from other parts of the world, I do not tremble in fear. It just takes a small change in life to make a big difference. That simple train trip to Madurai helped me overcome all my inhibitions about travelling alone to an unknown place.

However, not all challenges come in good faith. In my entrepreneurial career, I witnessed a classic case of gender discrimination and undue dominance of a male cofounder. There was a startup that was the brainchild of the female cofounder but the male cofounder held the majority of stakes. He was utterly dominating and demanding which was making the female partner lose confidence. She was far more talented than the man and he knew that well, so he always tried to cover his incompetence by dominating her in every facet of the business.

Lewd comments and uncanny remarks against a woman's achievements are such a common occurrence in almost every stratum of life. A woman is often belittled for her gender. The world ignores her achievements and concentrates on her limitations. Male chauvinism is a common element at workplace and it hinders the growth of a lady worker. Her performance is measured on a different scale than that of a man. Isn't this part of bullying? Of course, it is. Such undue dominance affects people mentally and it takes immense courage for a woman to deal with the working conditions where her talent is undervalued due to her gender.

Inappropriate behavior is omnipresent. One must know where to draw the line and one can do that only when one is aware of one's potential and flaws. Irrespective of your gender, age or professional background, your weapon to combat a bully is by breaking the chain of communication.

Once you stop paying attention or strategically start avoiding the person, you will be able to sideline every disturbing element that hinders your peace of mind. Tolerating ill-mannerism can never add any value to your life. It is all about setting priorities in life and realizing your true worth. Unwarranted demands do not always come in the form of bullying. Sometimes they just knock you down with incoherence and annoyance.

Let me share a weird incident from my life. I was nominated as a guest speaker at one of the events and I happened to reveal that joy to an acquaintance. He put forth a peculiar demand out of nowhere and asked me to request the panel members to nominate him as well. Now, how could I help him? Was I the decision-maker? No.

That person did know the reality and still pestered me for a while. Such inappropriate behavior is going to stand at your doorstep every now and then and you have to be prepared to say an emphatic NO whenever needed. Walking away from a situation with a NO is not an easy task. I could have said NO but I chose to rephrase my words suitably by putting the responsibility on the panelists. After all, they were the decision-makers.

However, there will be situations in life which you cannot escape this easily. Overly concerned parents who would not allow you to pursue your dream career, relatives who would like to take undue advantage of your professional life, and you will not know how to negate them. And then, there will be a bunch of people questioning your life choices, and another set would be waiting around the corner to pull you down. The trickiest part is how to react to such varied situations? I would say, place the ball in their court diplomatically. There is always a way to say no without uttering a NO.

Never Decline An Opportunity

When life is adamant to throw lemons at you, should you keep making only lemonade? Why don't you try some other recipes too? Hilarious, no?

Every problem that knocks at our door comes with two options. We can either accept the challenge to deal with something unknown or we can keep our door shut and remain hidden in our zone of comfort. Life is all about trading. I often feel overwhelmed by the kind of travelling I have to do. But then, every place I go to, I happen to learn something new and add another item to my list of achievements. Can I not restrict my achievements? Of course, I can. I have achieved quite a lot to live a peaceful life. I could have easily remained in my corporate job and that probably would have stopped many unwarranted questions. Probably I would have slept longer than what I do now. But seeking out opportunities amidst challenges is something ingrained in me. It is more like integrated within my DNA. I do not like to procrastinate for I know opportunities will be lost due to my reluctance.

Let me give the example of my MIT degree. I hatched that idea of pursuing the course in 2019 and did register for the program. Still, I was in a dilemma to pursue further as I was too occupied with my work and I was not sure if I would be able to finish off the assignments and travel to so many countries. Moreover, the course would have been possible at a later date as well; there was no need to hurry. Considering my prior commitments, I could have easily postponed the course for a couple of years. 2021 or 2022 would have been ideal. But I took the plunge and decided to work it out somehow. And today, when I ponder upon my decision, I do realize how right my decision was. Had I not opted before the pandemic struck, it would all have been a dream. I could easily finish the course before the Covid pandemic hit the world. The successful outcome was not caused by luck but by the courage to take the chance as and when it comes.

The future is always unfathomable; our plans can go awry without giving any prior intimation. And thus, it becomes imperative to understand the importance of time and chance. Coming to think of it today, the pandemic made me busier than before. Through that timely course of action, I realized that delaying something never solves anything for we can never know what future holds for us.

The tapestry of our life is woven with our dreams and desires. Not every dream may get fulfilled, not every desire can meet its fruitful end, but living under the protective sheath of comfort can never let you achieve anything in life.

Now, let me take you back to the same scenario where you wished to ride a gigantic wave. Can you do that by simply sitting at the beach and chanting your wish? No. You have to step inside the water first. You have to gather the courage to learn the tactics. Remember, you cannot learn swimming by watching a YouTube tutorial, you have to get into the water. You cannot be successful in life by reading others' success stories. You have to come to the battlefield to compete and showcase your potential.

In your pursuit of success, the most important element is your courage. Opportunities may seem to dry up and struggles may seem to raise their ugly head so much so that you wish to go back to your comfort zone. However, it is the element of courage that builds your confidence to move ahead in life. Your courage may not be visible to you every now and then, but believe me, we all have it within us, somewhere latent and ready to wake up right at the dawn of adverse situations.

> *"You gain strength, courage, and confidence by every experience in which you really stop to look fear in the face. You are able to say to yourself, 'I lived through this horror. I can take the next thing that comes along.' You must do the thing you think you cannot do."*
>
> – Eleanor Roosevelt

8

NOT ALL CLOUDS RAIN

"What I am against is false optimism: the notion either that things have to go well, or else that they tend to, or that the default condition of historical trajectories is characteristically beneficial in the long-run."

– Tony Judt

When I left the ever-prospering aisle of that corporate job, I carried an element of determination to make it big as an entrepreneur. When I found my father hesitating to disclose my plans of doing business, I made it a point to persevere so that I could bring back his confidence in my abilities. When the Shark Tank episodes roar on the TRP list, I am sure that every young mind sitting at the crossroad of choosing an appropriate career starts hatching this glamorous idea of becoming the next Flipkart or Nykaa. It sounds promising how media preaches about startups and their necessity in the current job market.

Moreover, who does not wish to create something unique in this world of gut-wrenching competition? Divergent is the need of the hour. The more unique you are, the better your chance to prosper. However, as an onlooker, you are witnessing only the tip of the iceberg. It looks small and easy to achieve, but the deeper you dig, you fathom the quagmire of risks associated with this line of action.

Entrepreneurship is more like the latest fever in the market, and apparently, almost every second aspiring young mind has been infected. Ask around, and people are ready to butt in with an innovative idea to bring a dramatic twist to India's growing economy. Considering the existing condition of the job deficiency, I do not see any harm in avoiding the sardined lanes of job seeking. After all, it is a matter of pride to transform from being a job-seeker to a job-giver. Amidst the job crisis, the glamourous side of entrepreneurship seems more alluring in a country like India because our startup ecosystem is flourishing well.

I often find the situation synonymous with the burgeoning enthusiasm for becoming a best-selling author. A few decades ago, when Chetan Bhagat and Amish Tripathi scripted their success stories as authors from a non-literature background, it set the market to new momentum. It injected a firm belief amongst the youngsters that every other soul has a story to tell and can invariably become an author while holding on to their full-time job.

And that has invariably become a reality. With so many publishing houses ready to launch budding writers, the dream has come true for many youngsters. But then again, the crowd of aspiring writers became so overwhelming that publishing houses became selective by scrutinizing the market value of the author. Well! Fair enough. After all, they are all here to do business and make money. Media showcased the success stories of those real achievers but always missed out on their struggles and the risk they had taken. The situation seems quite the same when the media flashes out the names of Ritesh Agarwal, Vijay Shekhar Sharma, and Binny Bansal. They are called the changemakers of the country.

They underline how much money they could mint while sublimely forgetting their struggles or the regular grind they go through even today. Every alternate day, there is news of a startup joining the unicorn bandwagon or filing for IPO. Media makes it look as if you wake up with an innovative idea, and then by the afternoon, one angel investor knocks at your door, makes your business roar, and by the next morning, you become a household name.

Does it happen so easily? Maybe when you spend your precious time daydreaming! Do you think every innovative idea is backed by a great business strategy? Huh! Ninety out of hundred startups fall flat within a couple of months due to poor planning. Believe me when I say this – the life of an entrepreneur does sound glamorous only when you are just ogling at the outcome. If you are bored of reporting to a boss, the concept of entrepreneurship will allure you with the flexibility it offers to build the type of company and work culture you like.

Moreover, as you watch the Shark Tank episodes, you are assured that the masses idolize successful entrepreneurs as they appear happier, more successful, and more driven than anyone else. Treading on the same note, have you ever visited the non-fiction section of a book store? Many books that boastfully sell the dream of business ownership will invite your attention. Somehow, I sense a touch of partiality in how entrepreneurship has been described and highlighted to the commoners. The reality is fabricated, or to put it accurately, you are force-fed with a half-baked truth. And still, hardly anyone tries to unveil the harsh realities to ignorant minds. I would like to quote Friedrich Nietzsche here – Sometimes, people don't want to hear the truth because they don't want their illusions destroyed.

Living In A Fool's Paradise

It feels good to dream of something big. After all, dreaming does not cost you anything—financial strain or physical anxiety.

The real prick comes when you take the first step to transforming your dream into reality. These days, everyone wants to try out entrepreneurship. Of course, some youngsters are brought up in a business-oriented household and invariably follow the legacy or start with something new. But that situation is starkly different from anyone and everyone willing to take the plunge into business.

I was new to the world of business when I decided to take the plunge. Having grown-up in a Bengali middle-class family, I could never weave the desire to be an entrepreneur. Entrepreneurship is a never-visited or prohibited zone for a working-class Indian, for we all are groomed with the idea of job security. Does entrepreneurship give you job security? No. How can you be secured when there is no guarantee of monthly income? Yes, there is no guarantee until your business picks up in the market.

While you weave the dream to be the next Mark Zuckerberg, you remain supremely ignorant of the darker shades of entrepreneurship. Behind the vibrant color of successful business enterprises, a murk of sacrifices and unimaginable compromises remain. While the media is busy showcasing the picture-perfect lives of successful entrepreneurs, there is a hidden dark side to being an entrepreneur that is rarely discussed. Moreover, none of you will believe it when I say that you have messed up the whole concept of entrepreneurship. Will you? Whenever an idea strikes us, it is our innate nature to link a successful personality with it. We learn something about the automobile industry, and our thoughts are immediately mesmerized by the success stories of Honda, Ford, and Suzuki. We hardly go through their tales of failures, for they do not seem to work wonders for our thought process. However, if you pay close attention to any successful businessman, you will be amazed by the struggles they face in their lives.

Do you know that Soichiro Honda had left schooling at the young age of 15? He became an apprentice at Art Shokai, an auto repair shop in Tokyo, and eight years later, he opened his branch of Art Shokai in Hamamatsu. In 1936, while he still worked at Art Shokai, Soichiro Honda created automotive parts for Toyota. They were rejected, though. However, that rejection did not deter him from his dreams. Soon after World War II, gasoline became scarce, and Honda offered a solution by creating a small 2-stroke motor that needed very little gas. It was designed for people to attach to their bicycles. By 1949, the Honda Motor Company was founded to launch the motorized bike.

It took another two decades for them to begin manufacturing cars. The world remains awestruck with those countless awards - Best Car of the Year; Top Safety Pick; Best Value Car, rarely does anyone think of the man's struggles. A great idea ignites the engine of entrepreneurship, but it is not enough to carry it forward.

The more you remain stuck to the glittering side of successful entrepreneurs, the more time you spend wandering in the fool's paradise. You have been so busy reading those select few stories of entrepreneurship — stories from the world of Tesla, Warren Buffet, Steve Jobs, Bill Gates, and Amazon, that you missed reading the stories of businesses like Blackberry, Blockbuster, Kodak, or Compaq. They were all billion-dollar enterprises that failed due to lack of innovation. Is it not ignoring the down side of entrepreneurship? You chose to scroll past the stories of Anthony Bourdain and Kate Spade who committed suicide. Why?

Let me wake you up from your dreamy world of entrepreneurship with the story about the death of VG Siddhartha, founder of CCD. The book of Entrepreneurship has many more chapters apart from multi-million-dollar business, funding, and a multi-million-dollar exit.

Wait! I am not demotivating you. I am trying to give you a reality check before you think of taking the plunge. The world has been cloaked in romanticizing the whole idea of entrepreneurship. It seems exciting to hatch and own an innovative idea and make it work in the world of business. Becoming your boss is indeed exhilarating, However, like every other endeavor, entrepreneurship comes with a bagful of unwarranted challenges that no one seems to perceive from the outside. When you believe in your idea and have decided to leave your job, you would not like to think about failures.

Even I did not know about failing, but I did strategize every step of mine, considering the perils associated with entrepreneurship. Many get so carried away by the promise of success that they vehemently deny the chances of failing and once they fall flat amid the increasing insecurities of this journey, they fail to cope up.

Even today, my friend who couldn't secure the funding for his startup is repaying the debts. What was his fault? He jumped the gun too quickly and started working on his business without securing enough funds. Today, he is still haunted by the failure of his first attempt at starting his own company and fears a similar situation rearing its ugly head if he tries again. Entrepreneurship is a risky affair. An idea that seems quite cool to you may not make any difference to society. You have developed an app that can help you decide on a meal you want to have. It sounds new and innovative that an AI guides you to decide on your meal. However, not many people would like to have an AI determine what they want to have.

Binging on a new idea is one thing, and making that idea work in the world of business is an entirely different story. Entrepreneurship is a constant grind where one wrong step can lead to a domino effect. You have to keep an informed mind and scrutinize everything on a larger scale. Apart from your great business idea, you have to look at the market scenario, competitors, and the growing ecosystem. Without comprehending the highs and lows of starting a business, every decision of yours will be hollow and futile.

"Business is always a struggle. There are always obstacles and competitors. There is never an open road except for the wide road that leads to failure. Every great success has always been achieved by fighting. Every winner has scars. The men who succeed are the efficient few. They are the few who have the ambition and willpower to develop themselves. So, choose to be among the few today."
— Chris Kirubi.

The Perils Overlooked

Entrepreneurship is all about risk-taking with a clear plan of action to launch a new product or service to fill a gap in the industry. If I take my example, the biggest risk I faced was to leave a stable job to launch a business. There was no guaranteed monthly income, no guarantee of success, and spending time with family and friends became a challenge in the early days of launching the company.

Businesses failing due to lack of focus are also well-known stories. Many young minds conceive a workable idea but lose focus in the middle of everything. You, as an entrepreneur, are a creator, not only of a product or service, but of your income. In case of entrepreneurship, sustained motivation along with patience, perseverance, and preparation remain the key to success.

Many young minds are overwhelmed by the number of options available, so they tend to nurture several ideas instead of focusing on one. Without setting your focus and prioritizing your tasks, how can you make a product successful in the market? Many startups have failed by getting tangled in too many things. However, falling is okay when you learn the lessons.

You fail to execute your ideas without focus, and you soon rectify your mistake. What if you become too focused? Most entrepreneurs invariably become workaholics because building something from scratch is a 24/7 job. Ambanis and Tatas were not built in one day. Every founder slogs day in and day out. Burning the midnight oil is part of entrepreneurial life, and if you are not prepared for that, do not step into this field. Time is money for every entrepreneur. In their efforts to utilize every second in building their business, they devote less time to sleep and leisure and may fall prey to depression.

Depression does not always come in the form of sadness. Sleep difficulties, irritability, and mood swings are common, making the entrepreneurs lead a life in isolation. Many entrepreneurs mask depressive symptoms by working longer hours and further worsening their emotional well-being. In one of the episodes of Shark Tank, Robert Herjavec revealed that he contemplated suicide.

It was indeed a courageous revelation that proves my point that fame, fortune, and success do not account for a peaceful life. More than anything else, it is inevitable for entrepreneurs to tie their self-worth to their net-worth. Over time, the business does not remain restricted to what they do, but it becomes who they are. When their business prospers, their self-esteem skyrockets, and whenever they lose a little money or fail in securing a target, they struggle with self-doubt.

Entrepreneurship thrives in a world where the biggies have proclaimed that failure is not an option, and such a notion has created a psychological crisis in the minds of budding entrepreneurs. Now, let us assume that your idea is great and you are focused and able enough to start a business. Can you wake up and create a company under your name? You will need funds to launch a business either in loans from investors or by using up a huge part of your savings. You have to put your hands in the fire. No matter how great your idea is, you should have a financial plan within the overall business plan. You should be ready to show income projections and the expected return for investors in the first five-year timeframe. If you fail to plan this accurately, no investor will be interested in joining in, and you too will end up in bankruptcy.

It was somewhere is 2002 and I remember having nothing in my wallet. I had to enter a Gurudwara langar to have my meal. Such situations are common. Entrepreneurship comes with a huge financial risk. The world perceives an entrepreneur as an innovative mind, but such a mind constantly struggles with anxiety.

The pressure of knowing that your ability to pay this month's EMI depends on closing the next deal or feeling that you cannot spend time with family because you have to keep working lends itself to incredible anxiety. Many entrepreneurs struggle to function because they remain worried about their business. Their strong desire to achieve can cause them to constantly contemplate worst-case scenarios. Eventually, the constant anxiety becomes immobilizing for many entrepreneurs and leads to burnout. A study published in the Journal of Business Venturing in 2014 found that habitual entrepreneurs display symptoms of behavioral addictions.

Obsessive thoughts, withdrawal-engagement cycles, and negative emotional outcomes are common. Emotional difficulties crop up in any kind of profession. Whether you wish to prosper in a luxurious cabin of a huge conglomerate or you want to stick to a meager job, success comes only after overcoming the hurdles. In case of entrepreneurship, the curve is deeper. A lot of factors are involved in making a business work.

The entrepreneurial lifestyle often lends itself to reduced resilience against mental health issues. The going often gets tougher beyond understanding, and many fail to cope with the fickle nature of this profession. However, that is the whole essence of the success stories. Never forget that Amazon started from a small cubicle, and it took them countless strategies to become a business giant. Unplanned meetings, unexpected struggles, sudden failures, and a full platter of risks, entrepreneurship encompasses all these apart from the success that you are shown.

Money Matters The Most

Our minds are trained to think that failure comes to those who are not consistent with their efforts. Take a leaflet from any entrepreneur's life book, successful or miserably failed, you will find a dedicated chapter on the daily grind. The struggle is inevitable, for you cannot mine a diamond without going inside a coal mine. Can you? A businessman is often considered to be richer than any salaried person. It is a notion that has been well fed through several generations. We imagine that a businessman has loads of money and gold. It may be true in many cases, but a common man often overlooks the risks a businessman takes.

Financial risk always lurks around the corner which in turn leads to emotional risk. While running the business, you realize that expenditure and revenue are two essential components but each carries a distinct tagline. Expenditure is more like a stone, and revenue is like a feather. Now imagine Galileo's experiment. What if someone throws expenditure and revenue from the 20th floor? The stone will reach you faster and hit you hard, while the feather will take its own sweet time to fall on your lap. Cash flow in business is as fickle as that feather. You will never know how long it will take for your business to profit. Doing business is not only about making money but investing a lot of money from your pocket. After all, you are building something that will feed many other people in the country. Finding a suitable investor is an arduous task.

Why would someone invest in you? There is a huge crowd of people serving better ideas every alternate day. There is a long queue of established businessmen you can trust easily for their experience in the market. Hardly any investor shows interest in budding minds who lack knowledge and experience. Also, even if you succeed in getting an investor and your business receives a kickstart, you cannot just sit and relax in the hope of seeing profits flushing in from every corner. It never happens like that. Financial planning is the most crucial element in doing business. Many entrepreneurs get trapped in misguided transactions and pay debts for the rest of their lives. At the same time, many others fall prey to showing off their trivial success, so they lose the whole essence of this long game.

The year 2020 witnessed the fall of one of the famous brands, Reid & Taylor (RTIL), when the company had to shut down its Mysore factory. The brand has been recognized for custom-made compelling first-class suits of top-quality exclusive materials. A company of Scottish origin had set shop in India and had established a name for itself across the country in the last few years. In 1998, S. Kumars obtained its ownership within India and started manufacturing and marketing for Reid & Taylor.

The deal initiated a luxury suiting plant at Mysore in 1998. An affiliate of GIC Special Investments acquired a 24.5% stake in Reid & Taylor with a valuation of US$121 million by 2008. However, the company kept incurring huge losses and was taken under the National Company Law Tribunal liquidation due to losses incurred in the past years. In 2020, things turned sour and the factory near Mysore was closed down leaving thousands of employees jobless.

The company was liquidated under the National Company Law Tribunal (NCLT) for bearing high non-payment loans. Moreover, they did not have any working capital to keep the operations going, resulting in the factory's closure and relieving all its employees from service. The company did not have any sale orders to execute, which led to continuous losses. The losses led to a lack of working capital to keep the operations active. Still, the company had survived for 14 months since the commencement of the liquidation.

But a lack of progress in business terms during that period led to further losses. Finally, the brand that was once represented by none other than Amitabh Bachchan suffered a shut down. It proves that money matters the most. It is the harsh reality of the business world. Poor calculation of funds, miscalculated investment, and ignorance of financial nitty-gritty often push most entrepreneurs towards an irreversible loss. When you have the entrepreneurial spirit, you should probably have a big picture of how your business would grow. You should have visualized yourself in next five or ten years. Having big dreams and goals is the key to success in entrepreneurship, but one must strike a balance between being realistic and going after big goals.

Most entrepreneurs in the big league often proclaim that one must be willing to dream big and take huge risks to see their business take off. However, it is up to you to decide the type and amount of risk you can afford to take. It is more like flying an aircraft. You cannot keep chasing the sky without paying attention to your fuel tank. What if the fuel ends in the middle of the flight?

While knitting some unrealistic dreams, you cannot abandon your family that has always remained by your side. If you check the entrepreneurial investment stories, you will find that most of the entrepreneurs had got initial funds from some family member or friends. You cannot run away with their hard-earned money. In your entrepreneurial journey, you will enjoy the favor of many helping hands, but only you can protect your growth. Your risk-taking appetite must not adversely affect others' well-being.

Risk is indeed crucial to entrepreneurial development, but the reality is that it is not just taking huge leaps without considering the options that make businesses work. Calculated risks are what make the businesses succeed. There is a big difference between taking a risk and taking a calculated risk, and the entrepreneurs who understand the difference make their mark in the field of business. In general, risk-takers do not keep in sight the escape route or the consequences of failure.

However, the entrepreneurs have to be mindful of effects of their actions as many things are at stake and this is where proper planning and strategizing every move play the most crucial role. Entrepreneurship fuels the idea of innovation and breaks the norm by introducing something new in the market. So, when you plan for something new, you cannot remain in the cocoon of comfort. You have to study the problem thoroughly to hatch the most suitable solution. But does the answer come in handy? No. If something is new in the market, it is bound to have a trial-and-error process, and there comes the need for any budding entrepreneur to take the risk.

"If you want to succeed at any level—in business, finance, and contribution to the world—you have to learn how to deal with this four-letter word: RISK."
– Tony Robbins.

Risk is an essential ingredient of success and thus, any youngster who wishes to plunge into entrepreneurship must be completely aware of it. Not everything that allures is productive; there prevails a fallacy in the world of entrepreneurship. Moreover, the glittering world of entrepreneurs has a brutal side of unfathomable struggle and random failures. If you wish to become the next Elon Musk or Jeff Bezos, you have to pay closer attention to their failed attempts and clever strategies. Success cannot be copied, for it carries a different connotation for different people. You may feel at the top of the world while running a small team of twenty people, whereas your friend may feel disgruntled even after making a million-dollar profit. So, it is all about perception.

Entrepreneurship is a long journey. From the stage of ideation to profit-making, it takes a gallon of patience and perseverance to sustain in the market, for there is a huge gang of people ready to topple you from your growth curve. Are you prepared for that? Right from the day you conceive the idea of starting a business of your own, you are liable to be judged on your insight. Some will criticize you for walking on an unfrequented path, and some will be ready to point out the flaws in your efforts.

There will always be someone to pull you down in the funding stage of a startup. I have faced several harsh comments just because the investor on the opposite side of the table was an MBA graduate from a great university. He knew almost nothing about entrepreneurial hardship but was eager to judge my business idea just because he was given the authority to question. But then again, many experienced people would benefit you with constructive criticism in order to help you grow further. Your chances of success improve with your ability to take the healthy criticism in the right spirit.

Failure in entrepreneurship is inevitable, and there is so escape from that regular grind. However, only this grind makes an entrepreneurial life worth living. I remember I was in Mumbai for a conference, and I had to stay overnight. I could not shell out much from my pocket as I was still nascent in my business. I decided to share the hotel room with one of my peers. Many incidents occurred when people tried to derive fun from my struggle, but I took everything in the right spirit. Every time I struggled, I felt motivated to reach my goal. Every day you are told that sky is the limit and you have to break that glass ceiling come what may.

> "No more romanticizing about how cool it is to be an entrepreneur. It's a struggle to save your company's life – and your skin – every day of the week."
> – Spencer Fry.

When you are standing at the dawn of your career, it is entirely up to you whether you want to be an entrepreneur or wish to be satisfied with a 9 to 5 job. In either case, life is not going to be easy. Struggles are a part of success, and while you get mesmerized by the glamourous lives of successful entrepreneurs, do not overlook the hardships they went through.

No success comes easy; no glamour arrives free of cost. Entrepreneurship is an uphill battle, and one must be prepared for the struggle before tasting the sweet nectar of success. However, nobody can force you to participate in this battle as entrepreneurship is not everyone's cup of tea.

Your ability to innovate and your readiness to take the risk is the first requirement. However, the better you study the market and opt for a suitable business model, the better are your chances of success. Tread on this path only if you value patience and determination and can face failure and criticism with an open mind.

9

STAYING CALM: A PRICELESS MANTRA

Who does not love cricket? For an Indian, cricket is not just a game but the essence of our secularism and patriotism. It is a thread that connects us all. The style, the aggression, the zeal dripping with pride of representing India; cricket binds us all.

In this gentleman's game, Rahul Dravid, popularly known as 'The Wall' of Indian Cricket is more like the calmness that precedes a storm. When I watch the CRED ad mocking his anger management issue, I am often reminded of his expressionless face when Shoaib Akhtar or Brett Lee used to spit some lewd comments. Hardly one would have seen him losing his temper during his playing days. He used to come to build a kind of shield over the wicket. He never bothered about how the bowler reacted; he just let his bat do the talking.

Indeed, Rahul Dravid rarely lost his cool even if there was an altercation with Michael Slater or he ran into Shoaib Akthar during the 2004 Champions Trophy. A few looks and snarls happened during those face-offs, but as soon as the bowler delivered the next ball, Rahul Dravid was back doing his best, crushing the bowler's ego with a solid defense.

We know the Newtonian law that every action has an equal and opposite reaction. So, whenever we are tempted or instigated by someone's untowardly actions, we react immediately to combat the effect of that action. No? However, if you sit and ponder, you will realize that not everyone or everything around you needs your immediate reaction. Sometimes, delaying your response weakens your opponent and gives you ample time to hone your strengths.

"To learn to see — to accustom the eye to calmness, to patience, and to allow things to come up to it; to defer judgment and acquire the habit of approaching and grasping an individual case from all sides is the first preparatory schooling of intellectuality. One must not respond immediately to a stimulus; one must acquire a command of the obstructing and isolating instincts."
— Friedrich Nietzsche.

Are you given a new assignment in an already packed schedule? The newly appointed lecturer enters the classroom, takes the piece of chalk, and writes 'Surprise Test' on the blackboard. Are you worried about your first date? Has your boss just reminded you of your crossed deadline in front of everyone? Has he just mocked you for not doing enough at work? These situations are far from rarity and appear irrespective of your age, chosen profession, gender, or anything. There are moments in life when you feel torn apart or caught between the devil and the deep blue sea, and you fail to fathom a way out of it. Your mind remains insulated inside a thick blanket of worries and anxiety, which never lets the problem go away; rather, you are kept reminded of the problem so often that you fail to concentrate on any other thing.

Difficult people or difficult situations create conflicting demands and make us feel terrible about ourselves. To think of it, none of us can alter a problem that has already rolled its ball to us. Neither can we change a person's attitude towards us? Toxic people are omnipresent, and it is more like their unpaid and unsaid job to pull others down. Nevertheless, a priceless mantra persists in dealing with such unwarranted chaos. Stay calm! No force can destabilize you once you start controlling your reactions.

Walking A Tightrope

Disappointment is finite, however, hope always runs around the infinity loop. Difficult situations come into everyone's life, and they metamorphose into different forms at different stages of life. Students appearing for their Board examinations find the throat-choking competition difficult to handle. They may spend hours and hours over a subject and still may not understand the core concept. Why? Students are so focused on the outcome that they overlook their scope of performing well most of the time. Students on the brink of adulthood, competing with their peers to get better marks, occasionally get bogged down when their performance does not meet their expectations. But why do they fail to meet their expectations even after spending so much time with their books? Half of the time, their mind is preoccupied with the worry of falling instead of working out a way to escape failure.

Similar situations crop up even for fresh graduates preparing for job interviews. Let us assume a hypothetical scenario. Rohit is a new graduate and is all set to appear for an interview at one of the best organizations in the country. He is well qualified and believes that he can clear the interview well. However, he is taken aback by those well-dressed and good-looking competitors. Somehow, his confidence wanes away, and he starts comparing himself with the others on the grounds that are not essential to getting the job. Even before he appears for the interview, he has accepted his failure for no good reason.

Whereas, another young man named Patrick participated in the interview on the same date. He is not a great student academically but quite comfortable and confident in his skin. He appears for the interview quite in control of himself. Now, whom do you think will be given the job? Both Rohit and Patrick are present in all of us. And it is entirely up to us whom we idolize in life.

We often lose our composure during difficult situations without realizing that the ability to manage our emotions under pressure or in a crisis is directly linked to our performance. Do you know that 90 percent of the top performers are skilled at managing their emotions in times of stress? They always remain calm and in control. The tricky thing about anxiety is that it is a necessary emotion. Our brains are wired, so it is difficult to take action until we feel comfortable in our emotional setup. But then, if you witness a high-performing individual, you will find him performing better under moderate stress because we humans need challenges to excel in life. A difficult situation or a toxic person often lets you unleash an unknown potential within you, but that can happen only when you accept the challenging position with a calm and composed mind.

Our ingrained habit is to always compare our status and achievements with others. Let us assume you are going to present your work in front of your colleagues. One question that keeps hovering over your head is 'Will I do well?'.

It is more like brewing self-doubt before even landing on the battlefield. You are more concerned about your looks, accent, and everything while forgetting the vital issue. It is a distraction as your mind ponders over something that is never under your control. These self-deprecating thoughts often get fueled when someone holding a position of authority points out our faults. Believe me when I say this – everyone has a problem with the other person. There is always a conflict of ideology where the person of higher repute considers them to be correct and infallible. When my startup was still growing, we invited a data analyst to have a look at our system. She spent a couple of hours and confidently declared that whatever our company had been doing was wrong.

She vehemently denied all the efforts my team had put in for the last six months by having a field trip for just a couple of hours.

Considering her educational qualification and professional insight, I could have kept quiet and accepted her version of the story. However, I let her speak fully and then asked her a simple question – How long did you spend on the groundwork? Initially, she was astounded as I did not provide her with any explanation for her blatant accusations. She gulped down a moment only to disclose that she had spent half a day. I contradicted again by clarifying that it was not even half a day but just two and a half hours. And before she could react, I responded calmly by posing a simple question – How can a few hours job give a more authentic picture when there have been people working for half a year to gather the ground reality.

Life takes just a fraction of a second to react to action; however, it takes level-headed thinking when planning to respond instead of reacting. A reaction hardly brings you the desired result, while a strategically planned response often bestows you with the upper hand in the situation. The moment you become comfortable in your skin and are well aware of your strengths and weaknesses, you can deal with any situation.

Let's take the same example of the guy named Rohit. He was well qualified for the job but lost his confidence after seeing so many candidates because he was unsure of his abilities. If I share a slice from my life, there have been several incidents where people tried to pull me down and expected me to deliver an immediate reaction. However, that has never been my nature.

Over the years, I have learned to hide my pawns. Once a team from Japan had come to inspect the kind of work iKure had been doing. After spending half a day, one lady from the group let out a deep sigh stating that it was nothing like what they had expected and that iKure should have organized it properly. I remember the day very well. It was quite warm, and we hadn't had any food till four in the evening. And this lady was not taking any break from complaining. I lent my ears till she was exhausted from her monologue.

And then, I politely asked if she ever lent a thought on the amount of hardwork we had been putting over the last six months.

Everyone was taken aback as no one in the room expected me to retort but politely. I am not advocating ill-mannerism here; however, I am urging the younger generation to be assured of their strengths so that no one ever takes you for granted. Instead of immediately reacting to a difficult person or a situation, let the opponents open all their cards. People suffering from superiority complex often live inside the bubble of an illusion. And that bubble can be pierced by well-planned strategic responses and not by immediate reactions.

Give Wings To Your Stress

"The ability to remain calm and focused in stressful situations is central to making positive decisions."
– Goldie Hawn

Life is competitive, and we all are running in the same rat race of doing better than the others. However, most of us nurture a habit of running away from challenges and taking an easier route to success. Avoiding a situation never equips you to handle it, but it proves your cowardice. Let us assume you have a presentation at your office. You are a little apprehensive as everyone in the gathering would be senior to you. Day in and day out, a chain of what-ifs haunts you.

What if you start stuttering? What if they all mock you? What if the boss does not like your performance, and you lose the job? Now, take a deep breath and ask one simple question to yourself. Are these what-ifs giving any benefits to you?

The answer is no. Instead of harping on what can go wrong, you can always practice your presentation in front of some of your good colleagues who would give you positive cues to improve yourself. Every stage in life is filled with some stressful moments. When you are a student, you are stressed about your exams, but worrying about the exam will not make you clear it.

As a job seeker, you are under stress about getting a job, and when you finally get a job, you stress again over your chances of promotion. Have you ever witnessed the last-minute preparation of a performer? Before going onto the stage, they never look at their lines, make-up, or costume. Rather they sit calm and composed, take some deep breaths, and remain blank for a moment. This whole routine gives their brain a relaxing moment to curtail all kinds of fear. The same principle works well in every facet of life. If you ever feel you are getting scared of a pending task, do not panic. Make a quick phone call to someone you love or trust. If you remain coiled in fear, you can never reach your ultimate potential.

Overthinking is one condition that always lurks in a young mind. For example, you are in your early twenties and are going on your first date. You take a couple of hours to decide on your dress, and even if you are looking good, you feel jittery. The more you concentrate on the date, the more fear you develop.

Instead, you can try to divert your attention to something more productive. Losing composure in such situations is common; however, practicing mindfulness can help you avoid this cluttering of your mind. Pull away from the problem for a while, even if only for an hour or two. When you give yourself time to process a dilemma and the surrounding emotions, you'll be able to approach the situation with a fresh perspective.

Whenever we encounter a serious situation, our first instinct is to panic. And if you continue to fall prey to severe anxiety and stress, you can have a complete meltdown. This response can cause long-term damage to your health and lower your ability to perform optimally.

Many of the world's greatest achievers, including entrepreneurs, athletes, and artists, could not have reached their level of success without realizing the significance of remaining calm under pressure. They can develop and maintain a particular state of psychological readiness, a mental preparedness they summon on demand. Whether you are an athlete, starting your career, or owning a company, poise is a prerequisite to peak performance.

And, you are poised for success when composed, sufficiently practiced, and self-assured. Very often, stress is cooked in the oven of our unorganized lifestyle. You have a well-paying job, and you are inherently talented to do justice to your role; however, you are thoroughly unprofessional when meeting deadlines. So, invariably every other client bang on your head because you fail to deliver your service on time. The more you see people questioning you, the more stressed you feel. Now, what is the solution? One of the easiest ways to give wings to your stress is by nurturing an organized lifestyle. Once your priorities are set, you can schedule your work and life properly and, in turn, can limit your stresses. You feel stressed when you are underprepared. You feel stressed when you keep thinking of failure rather than looking at the opportunity. You feel stressed when you are not sure of your abilities.

When stressful situations occur, your mind may wander in the aisles of negative thinking. The more your mind wanders, the more difficult it will be for you to remain calm. Stop yourself from beginning to imagine the worst-case scenario. Instead, let go of negative thoughts and refocus your mind on something positive, no matter how small. Take a break when you feel the situation is going out of your control. A 15-minute walk amidst nature lets you get some fresh air and opens up your mind. There are umpteen ways to manage stress and fight the chaos that runs errands inside our heads; however, nothing can beat the efficiency of a calm head.

Stress is the most common element amongst young achievers in today's fast-paced life, and they all have found ways to deal with it. The co-founder of ShopClues, Radhika Aggarwal, considers spending quality time with family as her biggest stressbuster. Catching up with her two sons over a good meal helps her keep her mind fresh. While for fitness-freak entrepreneurs like Keshav Bansal, there is no better way to relax than pumping iron, playing squash, and swimming. Mr. Bansal, the director of Intex Technologies, one of the top Indian handset makers which recently bought the Rajkot IPL team, ensures that he takes out adequate time every day to unwind.

He considers relaxing necessary to speed up one's progress. Bansal even finds time for a break between work — it may be a quick power nap or a brisk walk, or some deep breathing exercises. Such short and sweet breaks help in refreshing one's mind. They help in decluttering the mind and paves the path for having fresher perspectives.

Keeping Calm In Clamor

When you appear for an examination, no matter how good is your preparation, you are not assured of the outcome. There is a high probability of unwarranted situations cropping up from nowhere to stop you from achieving your goal.

Let me share another critical incident from my life. In one of my visits to Europe, I had a stopover at Milan, Italy. I got out of the aircraft to have some fresh air but was a little preoccupied with my thoughts. Unfortunately, I joined a queue which was meant for immigration; that is, for travelers who had the permit to enter the city. I, on the other hand, was a transit passenger and should not have got a stamp of permission into the city. The immigration officer was not attentive enough to check my papers and passport and simply stamped. I walked along and suddenly realized that I was no longer in the transit zone; rather, I was at the verge of entering the country without a valid visa.

Realizing my mistake, I joined the queue to enter back into the transit zone. However, hell broke on my head when the immigration officers suspected me to be a trespasser. I was taken inside a cell for interrogation where nearly ten officers kept pointing out the discrepancies in my papers and were adamant about blaming me for all the shortcomings. They kept asking about my European card, Italian visa and blah. It indeed felt scary. A foreign land, and there I was accused of something I had never done. I was a mere passenger fallen prey to a blunt mistake of an official. They kept stating several rules, one after another, to frighten me. But those rules were to be followed by the immigration officials at the desk.

I was a common man, and I should not have been bombarded with long lists of rules which their officials had failed to follow. I let the officer spit out everything he could.

But once he stopped, I just stated one simple line – *I am a transit passenger.* It was never a common man's mistake if the country's officials overlook the rules. The officials stamped on a passport without checking on the visa status. My calm and composed state of mind irked them further, and soon I realized that all this commotion was to cover up their mistakes. It was a serious crime and they wanted to trap me by making me accept an error that I had never committed. Initially, they were relentless, but once they found me not budging at all, they stepped back.

Life is loud and filled with clamor and commotion and there is no dearth of wrongdoers. If someone shouts at you and you yell back, raising of voice continues without offering any solution. One should combat the outcry with calmness. The calmer you remain, the less powerful the uncertain situations become. Many of you must have watched Sadhguru's sessions in his program *In Conversation with The Mystic.* During one such interaction, Manisha Koirala asked Sadhguru about something which all of us wish to have in life – the art of keeping calm in the clamor. Sadhguru said that if we are happy and peaceful only by accident, we will surely lose that state of mind.

The idea fits well for all of us. When we complain that life is full of challenges, we forget that our growth has been possible only by overcoming those challenges. Life runs on a cycle, much like any industry, and thus it can never be free of clamor. A life devoid of uncertainties and challenges will be boring and monochromic and believe me, no one can grow and prosper in a boring ambiance. We all need this clamor to know what we are capable of and understand our actual strengths and weaknesses.

However, the trick is to analyze the challenges without flustering. The outer world's noise must not make you lose your sanity because once you lose your temper, you let the difficult situation take control over you. The moment you can silence your inner chaos, we win over a tough situation. Consider yourself stuck in a traffic jam. An accident has happened, and traffic police has already told us that it would take another hour to bring the traffic back to normal.

Everyone is waiting patiently while you repeatedly honk for you have to reach your office for an important meeting. Everyone finds you weird as you lose your cool and spit abusive words about the system. However, nothing works out. The traffic clears after some time, and you reach your office on time. Still, you are no longer in a good frame of mind to make the meeting fruitful. Why? Because you had lost so much energy in the traffic jam. Your mind is cluttered now, and you fail to concentrate. What would have happened if you had remained calm? Your mind would have been fresh and stress-free for the meeting.

> *"Calm is the magic elixir that brings you to a place of balance, harmony, and peace."*
> – Donald Altman

Keeping calm is the ultimate mantra to lead a peaceful life. Once you learn to calm down the storm inside your head, you start enjoying the whole process of living. No one can control the challenges, for life is always inconsistent; however, everyone can control how they react to such challenging situations. Running away from difficult people or perplexing problems often appears as the easiest escape route, but then, if you keep running away, how can you make progress in life?

10

BAD PHASES: JUST A FEW PAUSES

Have you ever traveled by train and wondered how the outer sceneries change every minute? Your train runs through lush green fields, and the sky looks beautiful with the wisps of cottony clouds. You relax by the window rods and let the wind play around with your hair. However, even before you've been able to absorb the blissful moment, you feel your hands getting burned under the scorching Sun. You look outside and feel your eyes blinded by the bright sunlight. The breeze, the serenity, the soothing ambiance, all have vanished with no sign of coming back. You are thrown into an environment that you can neither like nor leave.

Life is exactly like that. Uncertain. Unpredictable with momentary doses of happiness and joy and then an unbearable bitterness of failures and hurdles. But then, life is not a straight road; it runs in a cycle where a bad phase is bound to be followed by a good one. A bad phase can be considered as a meaningful pause, a pause that will invariably leave us with a great lesson. Life is multi-hued, and every hue has its significance. Moreover, life is impartial.

It imparts a blend of good and bad phases in everyone's life irrespective of age, race, financial status, etc. Whether you are a famous cricketer or a successful businessman, life will be brutal and beautiful, and no one in this mortal world can do anything about it.

What is a bad phase? Well! That depends on who you are and what you are up to in life. If you are a student and fail to clear an important examination, that failure is a bad phase for you. If you are a young executive and all excited about an appraisal but do not get it, that brings a bad time in your life. Your age cannot act as a protective shield against a bad phase.

What if you are professionally very successful but fail in making any personal relationship work? There is no guarantee of protection from bad phases; we all fall prey to such drastic times in life at some point or the other. On the same note, we being mere humans, it is our intrinsic nature to seek advice or solace from others. There is nothing wrong with that; we are born to be social beings. However, seeking comfort from the outer world is often tagged as a sign of weakness in most cases.

Let us assume a hypothetical case scenario. You have been working in a big corporation. One fine day, you decide to plunge into the world of entrepreneurship. You take a leap of faith and start your business, but in a few months, you incur huge losses.

Of course, your close friends and family come for your support; however, in due time, they step back as everyone has their own share of worries. No one can be by your side 24 by 7, consoling you about your failed attempts. After a point in time, you will have to stand for yourself, which is the fact of life. Moreover, as you move ahead in life, you will realize that failures and setbacks are a regular affair. A friend who comes to your rescue once may not be available the next time.

Does that mean the friend is no longer a friend? No. It simply means that you have to get up on your own every time you fall and move ahead. A helping hand is what we all need sometimes but it cannot be made available all the time.

> *"The difference between darkness and brightness is how you thrive on those moments and use such circumstances with goodwill in your spirit."*
> — Angelica Hopes

This Too Shall Pass

It sounds cliched. But believe me, there is no bigger truth than this. If the present moment has gifted you glory and success, the moment will pass away soon. On the same note, if you are exhausted from repeated failures, even that routine will change. Change is inevitable and the only constant in our life. A bad phase, too, shall slip out of your grip. However, nothing happens on its own.

Some of the critical moments in our life are crafted on the foundation of failures and setbacks and we all do feel the need for one helping hand in such times. We need to have friends and family by our side whenever we bite the dust. However, more than any external support, our courage is required to fight back the bad phases in life. Consider yourself failing to get a suitable job even after getting a degree in flying colors. Of course, you feel low, and your self-esteem takes a beating in any public gathering. However, the more you feel ashamed of yourself, the more you withdraw yourself from the world, and the more it will hurt.

Let's say your mother is consoling you and encouraging you now and then. Your friends are also looking out for different opportunities suitable for you to kickstart your career. But, can you achieve anything by simply sitting and listening to their consoling words? No. You have to stand up for yourself and fight your own battle. If you fail in one interview, you should garner the courage to face another, for there is no other way to get a job. Doing well and still failing is a part and parcel of life.

If I take my example, I could not crack the IIT entrance, and it was a shattering experience in my life. There was a small pond behind our house, and I remember spending hours sitting idle over there, pondering upon my future. Millions of doubts cropped up, and success and failure took different avatars at different phases of my life. However, the only thing that kept me agile and moving was my courage and determination. Going numb during the darkest of hours is a common response. We are humans, and setbacks kindle an emotional turmoil more than anything else.

However, there is a small trick to handle setbacks. Once you disclose the news of your failure to the world, you enhance your vulnerability. While building my company, I had several setbacks and was very often assailed by unwarranted changes. One of the greatest mantras to deal with bad phases is never to disclose all your plans. The more you talk to people about your problems, the weaker you become. Instead of narrating your problems to hundreds of people, it is better to discuss the solutions with a few. No?

When problems knock at our door, we do get an option to escape from them and get cocooned inside our comfort zone. If I look back in life, when I had no money to eat a decent meal, and I had sat down for a free dinner at the Langar, I did have the option to call my father and seek monetary help from him. However, that phase of eating a free meal out of desperate need kindled a kind of new zeal. I was more determined to achieve my goals and that would not have been possible if I had sought my father's help during that difficult phase. The darkest hours in life often push us to work harder in search of that ray of hope.

Have you ever been without money? Let's say your laptop is very old and you have been struggling to finish your assignments on time. You are good at studies, but the outdated system hinders your progress. Can you buy the latest model of laptop now? You take a pause and think of possible options. Either you can ask for money from your parents; however, a computer does not cost a mere thousand rupees. Your middle-class parent may not be able to spend so much money on your new need. You realize that you have enough free time to opt for a part-time job. In a couple of attempts, you get a part-time engagement and soon make some money to get a laptop, at least on an EMI basis.

Now, why did you never think of this part-time job before? Because earlier, there was no shortage of money to fulfill your basic need. As you fall prey to hardship, your mind automatically goes into a solution-searching mode. Your mind walks through all the options available, and your courage, determination, and confidence let you choose a suitable path to success.

There arrive many difficult situations in our life. We are fulfilling our basic needs, cost of education, cost of living, paying EMIs, and whatnot. We are rummaged by thousands of problems at every stage in life, and soon fear takes birth. Every day, we are haunted by self-doubts. What if I fail to pay the monthly rent? What if my medical bills cross the limit?

While we invest our time in these what-ifs, we feed our vulnerability. The energy we invest in worrying about the problem goes waste if we don't intend to seek any solution. When we keep thinking about the situation, our brain gets focused only on that one problem losing sight of all the other opportunities. A problem is never a loner. It is imperative to look at the problem and its solution as a couple.

I started working for a website after the langar episode. It was somewhere between 2002-2003, and I was offered around 9000 rupees for an assignment. My determination to fill my wallet was so strong that I started the work at 10 o'clock at night and finished it by 7 o'clock in the morning. Even today, after so many years, I don't know how I could complete the work so efficiently. I believe a fighting spirit takes birth when you decide to combat a difficult situation. Every difficulty, every hurdle gives birth to a new process that helps us evolve in life. But then, nobody likes problems, and everyone strives to avoid difficult situations, and yet, the real essence of life lies in facing these challenges head-on and emerging victorious.

> *"I don't run away from a challenge because I am afraid. Instead, I run towards it because the only way to escape fear is to trample it beneath your foot."*
> – Nadia Comaneci

The Escape Velocity We All Need

Escape velocity is perhaps our high school companion. We bunked many lectures while mocking the Earth's gravitation.

However, the concept of escape velocity becomes relevant when we deal with bad phases in life. What does a bad phase do? It pulls us down. A wrong step is analogous to gravitational pull, which tries to hold us tight amidst all the problems. But, if you look from the perspective of Physics perspective, we all can apply escape velocity to come out of the clutches of a problem. Now, where does this escape velocity dwell? It resides inside our head. Our willpower to overcome a bad phase is the fuel to power that escape velocity.

The idea is not to escape or run away from the problem. It is about escaping the problem by solving it. Is it that easy to stand up against a problem? Let us analyze the situation with our body's immune system. Whenever we suffer from an infection or a physical injury, the white blood cells of our body rush to the site of the injury to mend the damage. They do not wander anywhere else but only towards the site of injury or infection. This targeted move is not to dissect the wound but to heal it.

Similarly, whenever we encounter a problem, our mind and body should focus on finding the solution. Just think once. When you fall and injure your knees or any other part of the body, people around you come to console you or invest their time looking after you. However, the injury is healed by medicines and proper treatment only. Bad phases too, can be overcome by appropriate actions and not by mere consolation.

The human mind is inherently weak. Whenever we fail or encounter a bad phase, our mind takes refuge in the darkness of negative thoughts. We keep thinking of others' judgments about our failed attempts. Whether you failed in a job interview, missed a promotion, or fell flat in your attempts at entrepreneurship, you keep thinking about people's judgment.

Even when you try to chalk out a plan to overcome the hurdles, you lend an ear to what others think. Why? People will talk. The world is opinionated. We all harbor a particular perspective towards everything, be it success or failure. However, if the bad phase revolves around you, only you have to get up and face it.

People can inspire you to choose a particular path, but it is up to you to walk towards the solution. Let us think of the physical injury again. We often bandage a wound. Why? Because healing can happen only inside you. Whether you are going through physical pain or emotional turmoil, the healing process starts and ends within you, not in the outer world. I am a firm believer in having all options open. Even if I am sure that Plan A works wonders, I keep a Plan B ready.

The term 'Bad Phase' may seem universal; however, the steps one takes to come out of that bad phase are not the same for everyone. What worked for me may not work for you at all. Does it mean that there is no other way at all? No. While you strive to find a solution to a problem, you must be prepared to keep digging. If one plan does not work, you have to move to the next plan, and the process must continue until you solve the issue. Problems or bad phases do not come to us to drown us into them. They come to make us think deeper and develop a new perspective altogether.

They say God helps those who help themselves. The focus of this proverb lies in the tail segment. You have to work hard to get things done. Sitting in your comfort zone and constantly nagging about the problem will not let any miracle happen. Let us assume you have a bad boss at work. It becomes exhausting to wake up every morning and face the same problematic work environment every day. At one point in time, you reach the threshold of bearing the pain. Can you keep suffering like this? No. It is insane and inhuman too. You must stand up against the problem while maintaining your calm. Initially, your concern may not draw anyone's attention, but gradually people around will understand and rectify the issue.

Similarly, we may encounter a difficult situation due to our misdeed or mistake. We can always sort it out by talking. Whether it is the miffed boss or a troubled relationship, things always work out if we open up about the situation. There is no harm in taking the first step. There is no harm in apologizing for your mistakes. Once we are open to solving a problem, we automatically move towards having a productive solution.

Moreover, once we know the cause of a problem, we can always avoid making the same mistake. Most of the difficult situations crop up due to our miscalculations and heightened expectations.

Let me share another incident from my life. It was 2013-14 and my team expected to win the first prize of around five lakh rupees. The amount was significant, and winning could have added to our confidence as a budding company. However, we lost, and it broke me down. It is natural for any person to lose faith when the outcome does not meet expectations. The program was in Manesar, and when my team lost the deal, I felt so low that I went to have some lone time in a temple. I gathered my confidence the next morning, went for a walk, listened to music, and chalked out a plan to improve myself. Whether the winner deserved the prize or I merited to be treated better or not was no longer my consideration for I had moved on with life.

We all are aware of Elon Musk's repeated failures at SpaceX. In many interviews, Musk has disclosed how he was asked to step back from his dream project. However, he remained persistent and soon tasted the sweet nectar of success. No one can overcome a hurdle without trying to fight back. Patience, persistence, and perseverance are the key factors in dealing with limitations.

The Problem With Heightened Expectations

A couple of years ago, I was invited to attend a program in Jaipur. Somehow, it had been a busy day, and I could not have a proper meal. Even on the flight, I just managed with some cashew nuts and biscuits, presuming that the event would have an elaborate dining facility. That was my expectation. When I landed in the middle of the lunch hour, I was informed that there was no arrangement for lunch. I was given an option to have lunch in their usual canteen. Unfortunately, the quality of food and the ambiance of the canteen were too bad, and I could not accept that. I went through physical and emotional turmoil and, within a couple of days, fell sick. My over-expectation had caused most of the problem.

Let us consider the case of a new employee. He has entered the company and everyone appreciates his work and his positive approach to everything. He feels special, but people stop showering him with extra attention after some time. What should he do? Should he feel left out? His feelings have nothing to do with his career and growth curve. He cannot expect his colleagues to overlook his mistakes time and again and if people's altered attitude towards him bogs him down, the problem lies in his expectations. He cannot expect to be the center of attraction all the time. Not everyone will come to him and befriend him. He too has to make a move and lower his expectations in life.

Once you improve your reality and lower your expectations, you move closer to happiness. We all try to fit people and situations within our frame of expectations and when they don't fit in, we feel bad. Being myopic in your perspective is never helpful when you wish to grow in life.

Bad phases come as a learning period. Even when you struggle to make ends meet, you learn different ways of survival. Every time you fail an examination or job interview, you learn a new way to answer the critical questions. Every time a relationship goes through trouble, you become a better person. Bad phases are those pauses in which we look back at life to understand what went wrong and how to correct it.

"Life is a series of experiences, each of which makes us bigger, even though sometimes it is hard to realize this. The world was built to develop character, and we must learn that the setbacks and grieves we endure help us march onward."
– Henry Ford

Failures, setbacks, disappointments, and bad phases are sometimes blessings in disguise. They come to enhance our determination and plant a seed of dedication towards our ultimate goal. Your ability to face setbacks and failures is a measure of your ability to succeed.

Life presents us with both stepping stones and stumbling blocks, and it all depends on how we perceive every episode of life. We can make failures a part of our success story or use them as excuses for taking the exit route. Only a winning attitude can make us move ahead in life. Bad phases are inevitable and your success and contentment depend on how you face them.

CONCLUSION

Life moves on. Whether you weave a beautiful tapestry of dreams and desires or come to naught, life moves on. Whether you get going even after repeated failings or take refuge in the comfort zone of doing nothing, life marches ahead. Life is uncertain, unpredictable and always keen on throwing obscure challenges at us. None of us are given any script of life to be prepared for the future uncertainties, but we all are given fair chances to learn the tactics of life. In the middle of the night, if you are chased by a pack of dogs, you need to strategize your next move, for there is no guardian angel coming to your rescue.

We often wander in the aisle of doubts questioning the very need of challenges in life. Challenges have only one role; they come to test our courage and confidence. We are often stuck in the same cycle of life for we fail to look beyond our comfort zone. We often fail to comprehend the need for connecting with people, the art of persuasion and the pure magic of making use of every opportunity in life. As we fail to achieve our goals, we tend to sink in the pool of depression. We desire to become something, but fall prey to societal demands, parental influences and often indulge in the same monochromic life. Why?

Because, we fail to make people understand our true nature, our deepest desires and our inherent ability to win over challenges. We fail to look at the significance of building emotional connections with people amidst the chaos of social networking. The idea of befriending a stranger sounds cooler and more efficient in real life than on virtual networks. The art of persuasion and our ability to build long lasting relationships are the key to success. And while we think of success, knowledge is our weapon. Gather knowledge in whatever way possible. Invest time in accumulating knowledge.

Living in the 21st century is demanding as we are thrown into plethora of challenges and pitfalls. Every second youngster is a victim of depression for they fail to come out of the pit of failure. We have to understand that failure is a part of life and there is no escape route. Even if you fail a hundred times, you have to get up and get going. Even if you fail to crack an important examination in life, you have to think out of the box and find a different opportunity to flourish in life.

Today, as every young mind is zealous about entrepreneurship, they must analyze the complete picture of success and failure. In your chase to build your own business empire, you should be prepared for the unwarranted demands of life. All that glitters is not gold. The basket of life carries the cheers of success and greys of failure and we cannot be selective while making our picks. If we desire to be successful, we have to walk over the thorns of failure as well.

When things do not work our way, when people around mock us for our incapacities, when someone basks in their superiority complex and bullies us, we just have to keep calm. A quiet head is a storehouse of solutions. No phase in life is permanent. Good days wane out and so do the bad days. It is our patience, perseverance and persistence that remain forever. Yes, life is a race and we all have our own tracks, own rules and own destination. Do you know why challenges in life are referred to as hurdles? Because there is always a way to overcome them.

Success and failure are two sides of a coin and you have to flip the coin again whenever it falls on the side of failure. It is okay to fail, as failures make us unleash our true potential and see through the veiled opportunities. All we need is a tenacious grip over our goals in life. Once the goal is set, we learn every facet of life and find out new ways to achieve our milestone.

"Every defeat, every heartbreak, every loss, contains its own seed, its own lesson on how to improve your performance the next time."
– Og Mandino

Dear Readers,

Thank you for making this book a part of your life! Even though you have reached the end of the book, this is not the end of our journey together. It's just the beginning! A plethora of opportunities are waiting for you to be explored that we would like to give you as a parting gift.

iKure is coming up with its own Community Research Facility aka The Living Lab in Baruipur, West Bengal. The architecture which has already been done by HDR in association with a New York top architectural firm. This project is supported by **Construction for Change (CFC)** which is a Seattle, United States based organization and **Srijan Realty (a real-estate agency)** based in India.

The Living Lab will serve as a platform of collaborative ecosystem that will bring in the Researchers, Academicians, Students, Scientists and Doctors from all round the world into one platform thus opening a door for learning, creation and innovation.

What will be your takeaways?

- Learnings through webinars and expert academic sessions.
- First hand experiences in working with Researchers & World Class Academicians because we all know books aren't enough.
- Community based Research for projects/surveys/thesis.
- Learning to network & building relationships.

This is a once in a lifetime opportunity that iKure is giving to all my readers. You would miss out a great deal if you don't scan the QR code below. Behind the QR code, lies a door of fun learning experiences & opportunity to innovate for you all. So come join us and be a part of this wonderful experience.

Register yourselves by just scanning the QR code:

www.ingramcontent.com/pod-product-compliance
Lightning Source LLC
Chambersburg PA
CBHW022359040426
42450CB00005B/247